From Loss to Living
WOMEN LIKE ME

Compiled by Julie Fairhurst

WOMEN LIKE ME

From Loss to Living

JULIE FAIRHURST

Rock Star Publishing

COMPILED BY JULIE FAIRHURST

At times, some readers may be triggered by a women's story. Should you need to speak with someone, there are many crisis lines, counselors, and doctors that you can reach out too. Find someone that can lend a kind ear to listen to you. That can be a friend, parent, spouse, or anyone that you trust. Your local community services may have telephone numbers to assist you.

www.womenlikemestories.com
Rock Star Publishing

Contents

...

Maya Angelou

"We delight in the beauty of the butterfly, but rarely admit the changes it has gone through to achieve that beauty."

Introduction

How often do we hear of others who experience loss, allowing it to overtake their lives? Not everyone overcomes loss, and they can live with it forever.

Loss can come in many forms...

Death of a loved one

Being let go from a job

Child custody

Financial

Divorce

Friendships

Independence

Death of a family pet

Health

Grieving your loss is a process that has to take place in order for healing to happen. And it takes time. How much time? Well, that would depend on the individual.

The eleven women who have written in this book, Women Like Me - From Loss To Living have dealt with overwhelming loss in their lives. Each dealing with it in their individual way. However, they dealt with it, in the end, they were able to overcome it, move forward, and start living again.

These incredible ladies are sharing their stories in the hope that you, the reader will find comfort, peace, and inspiration to move forward in your life. It was a healing experience for them, to tell their story. When we keep our stories lock up in our hearts and minds, negative emotions will eat away at our souls. We need to release negative emotions.

Anger, resentment, sadness, despair, and guilt are common emotions that a person dealing with loss can experience. And, that is okay, these emotions are normal and a process that most will go through. But what is not okay, is to allow those emotions to stay with you for years and years, never healing from your loss.

Those negative emotions will eventually come to the surface and when they do, they may manifest as illness and affect your health. We can't keep them stuffed down forever. One day they will come to the surface.

You may experience trouble sleeping or you sleep all the time. You may develop a lack of appetite or overindulge. Turn to substances like drugs and alcohol to numb what you are feeling. Being tired all the time and crying for no reason. You may find you are shutting yourself away and refusing to see your loved ones.

These are common coping mechanisms that many of us will use to push away dealing with our loss. But pushing it away, will not solve anything, and make the situation worse.

As you read the stories of these strong women, who knew they had to deal with their loss in order to live a better, fuller life, we hope you will move towards healing, as they did.

You may want to start to journal about your loss. Write whatever comes to your mind and get it onto paper. There is a healing that takes place when you write. It is a release.

If you feel you need help to heal, then reach out to a professional that can help. Share your feelings with a trusted loved one, who supports you. Releasing your loss is imperative for your well-being and happiness. Be strong for yourself, reach out.

And take care of yourself. We, women tend to put ourselves on the back burner and put everyone else's needs ahead of ours. This is a terrible way to live your life. Think about it! If you are not healthy, emotionally, physically, and spiritually, how can you take care of others properly?

I'm not talking about neglecting your responsibilities. I'm talking about knowing your worth and your place in the world. Women are the light for their family, but if your light is burnt out, no one will have the light. Take care of yourself, so your light can continue to be bright and shine on those you love.

Much love and happiness to you,

Julie Fairhurst, Founder of Women Like Me

...

Trisha Yearwood

"What's meant to be will always find a way"

PART I

From Loss to Living

A Moment in Time
LIFE WILL NEVER BE THE SAME

"People stare like they've never seen a goddess in a wheelchair before." - Sydney Mickey

W hen I looked at my rear-view mirror, I felt immediate panic. I couldn't find my voice to say what I saw, and my hands gripped the wheel so intensely that they throbbed. I looked over my shoulder to let them pass, but what happened next changed our lives forever.

April 24th, 2016, was one of the most traumatic experiences I've ever encountered in my life. I remember the day so perfectly. It was a surprisingly sunny day in the normally rainy town of Prince Rupert. I woke up in my home with my beautiful family I created with my son's father, Shane. He was asleep on our bed while I played with our two-month-old son and our dog, Biggie.

My son's grandma, Sylvia, wanted to take the baby for the day, so we drove to his grandma to drop him off, and I told my baby I'd see him soon. We normally would take our dog everywhere with us, but that day, we decided to leave him home for some reason. Shane and I decided that we'd take advantage of the beautiful day and drive to the lake. We picked Shane's cousin up before we went on the highway to the lake, which was about 15 minutes out of town.

Shane wanted to drive, but there was nowhere to pull over; therefore, we'd have to wait to switch spots at the rest stop five minutes out of town. We were listening to music when I noticed a blue car swerving in my rear-view mirror. I knew they had to be drunk because they were driving so recklessly on the one-lane, two-way highway.

My heart began racing, my palms sweating, and I gripped the steering wheel so hard that my hands were throbbing. I was so afraid that I couldn't find my voice to tell Shane that the people behind us were drunk. We were just around the corner from Oliver Lake when the blue car swerved into the other lane to pass me. When I thought they'd be gone soon, I felt relieved. I began to slow my vehicle down to let them pass, but when I looked over my shoulder, I saw their car ram into mine before we drove into the ditch.

When we came to, Shane asked us if we were okay, but I was unsure. He climbed out of the car through his window and was immediately horrified by the seriousness of the crash. I was stuck between the windshield and crushed hood of my car, unable to move. When I tried to move my legs but couldn't, I knew immediately that I was paralyzed. The adrenaline was pumping through me, so I didn't quite understand the severity of it all.

I remember my neck felt extremely uncomfortable, and I tried to push my head out. Shane was hysterical, saying he couldn't believe this was happening. The four people in the other car jumped out, and one of them jumped on the hood of my car to ask if everyone was okay. When he jumped on my car, I felt extreme pressure on my neck, and Shane told him to get away from us because he was hurting me.

A paramedic who was off duty at the time had seen the whole crash unravel and came to help. He assured me that help was on the way, though it felt like ages before they arrived. It was music to my ears when I heard the sirens. I felt relieved knowing that I'd be in good hands soon.

When the firefighters and paramedics analyzed the situation, they realized that the car's roof would need to come off to get me out safely. They needed to use the jaws of life to take the roof off in order for me to be removed from the windshield safely. I remember how loud and terrifying it sounded when they were cutting the metal that trapped me. Once it was off, I fell back slowly while about five or six people kept my neck and head steady. I remember looking up at the beautiful, blue, cloudless sky while they carried me out of the ditch. I blacked out shortly after getting into the ambulance.

I was medevac from Prince Rupert to Vancouver General Hospital by helicopter, although the only thing I remember is throwing up in the helicopter before blacking out again. I had to undergo multiple surgeries, including hardware being put into my neck to stabilize it and a tracheostomy, so I was able to breathe through a ventilator and a metal plate in my wrist because it was shattered. My mother explained to me that the x-ray of my wrist looked like someone twisted it around and then squished it together.

Each surgery was roughly nine hours or more. I was put into a drug-induced coma for five days to let my body heal from all the traumas. During that time, I had an allergic reaction to one of the drugs they gave me, and it made me really sick. I had a high fever which was hard for my body to fight. They weren't sure if I would make it, so my dad (who doesn't believe in religion) prayed to the higher power to heal me. The next day, I was doing so much better and went into recovery.

Once I woke up, I remember my cousin, Natasha, telling me that I was in a car accident. And I was thinking, "Wow, that was so long ago. Why are people still talking about it?" I didn't understand where I was or the severity of my injuries. I was heavily medicated and hallucinating to the point where I was 100% sure that the nurses in VGH were trying to steal my lung to give it to their relative. It felt like I was running all over the lower mainland, trying to get away from them, but they kept finding me. I would try to tell my family members when they'd come to see me; however, they couldn't understand me. It was so surreal. It still feels like it happened even though I know that was hallucinations.

I had to stay in the Intensive Care Unit (ICU) for nearly a month. During that time, I couldn't hug or kiss my son. He couldn't visit much because I had an infection, and everyone who entered my room needed to wear Personal Protective Equipment (PPE).

I spent my first mothers day in the ICU. Thankfully Shane and my parents brought him to see me briefly. On May 15th, 2016, I was moved out of the ICU and onto the Spinal Unit located on the 9th floor in Vancouver General Hospital.

I was really groggy during my time in the ICU, but when I moved to the Spinal Unit is when I started working aggressively to get better and transition into this new life. I would do "breathing trials," which was when I would be taken off the ventilator and needed to breathe on my own for a period of time—each time being longer than before. It absolutely exhausted my energy because it was hard after not being able to breathe on my own for so long.

After seven weeks of being in the hospital, the cast on my wrist was able to come off. I was cleared by the doctors to put pressure on it, and that's when my physiotherapy began. I needed to learn to do everything all over again, so my son and I shared a lot of milestones together. We learned to sit up around the same time, I remember during one physio session Kayden, and I were holding each other up and balancing gracefully.

After three months of not eating or talking, I could breathe independently and only needed the vent while I slept. We shared honeydew melon together when I was finally able to eat.

In July, I was transferred to G.F. Strong Rehabilitation Center, a place where they would help me transition into my new life with a C7 spinal cord injury. They helped me regain most of the movement in my hands, about 65%. They taught me the basic necessities for everyday life, such as cooking, grabbing stuff off the ground, getting in and out of bed, etc. By November 22nd, 2016, I was discharged from there and moved to Surrey with my mom, my dad Wilfred, my three sisters, and my son; I lived with them for two years while they helped me with what they could to make this new life easier on me.

It was hard adjusting to my new life. There were many days, weeks, and months where I felt like I couldn't go on like I'd be better off dead. I was filled with anger. I despised the people who ignorantly drank and drove, taking away the future I had planned before being permanently stuck in a wheelchair. I had my independence taken from me. I never thought I'd get it back. I was adamant that I didn't want to drive ever again. I figured I'd just use transit or rely on others to help me.

That lasted about ten months before I reached out to start Drivers Rehab and learn to drive with hand controls. On May 25th, 2017, I drove for the first time. It felt amazing. From then on, I completed ten sessions of Drivers Rehab and was officially able to drive on my own. It was hard driving on a highway. Even now, in 2022, I get major anxiety on the highway. It was a lot to adjust to, but I am so glad I did.

After two years, the woman who hit me, Megan, was finally charged. We were supposed to go to trial until she pleaded guilty; therefore, we got a sentencing date for November 2018. She had lost herself in addiction. She was living right on the downtown East Hastings Street in East Vancouver. She was severely addicted to drugs which unfortunately came before her kids, family, and our court proceedings. She missed many court dates, but they kept letting her out shortly after arresting her; it was infuriating.

I hated her for not only changing my life but also skipping court appearances was a slap in the face. I didn't realize that she was probably hurting and ashamed to face what she did. She was arrested on June 17th, 2019, and remained in jail until the sentencing date on August 30th, 2019. I had to fly to Prince Rupert for court. She stayed in the lower mainland jail because she refused to travel to court. I'm assuming because of being ashamed.

I rolled into the courtroom with the amazing support of my friends and family. I was ready to leave this chapter in my life even though I hated Megan so much and wasn't about to change my mind. When I was in the courtroom, I read my six-page Victim Impact Statement without shedding a tear in court.

After hearing what Megan had to say, we took a lunch break. I turned to the prosecutor and started crying because I wanted to tell Megan something that I never thought I could ever say or do. We returned after lunch, and I finally told her, "I forgive you; I forgive you for everything you've done and caused. I hope one day you're able to forgive yourself. My son didn't lose his mommy, so her sons shouldn't lose theirs. I hope you embrace the tools in jail to get sober and clean, and I hope one day you can repair the broken bond with your sons."

Everyone was shocked. I had been carrying around the burden, the baggage that wasn't mine to carry. I gave it back to her and felt immediately freed from the hate and anger I felt for her. The judge sentenced her to 18 months, but with time served and only serving two-thirds of her sentence, she was released almost eight months later. Everyone was upset, but I reassured them that there was no reason to be upset. For her to get any jail time was good enough for me.

I've learned so much about myself in the six years since it happened.

I still remember the days without independence, thinking I'd never get that back. It's incredible to reflect on because I am so independent now, I bought my own home in 2021, and it's perfect. It was already modified for a wheelchair before I bought it, so it's perfect for my grandparents, my son, and me. I have been through hell and back, I've gone through trauma after trauma, and I'm so glad I'm able to write about one of them.

I still struggle daily, but my life has actually gotten better than before the accident. With that being said, SPEAK UP AND SPEAK LOUD when you see ANYONE about to drink and drive, take their keys, call the cops, and do whatever you can to ensure they get home safely without driving. This could happen to anyone, and it has to countless people who are the victims of drinking and driving.

Believe me. It isn't worth it; so many lives were changed on April 24th, 2016, and we lost our old lives that day. Over something that could have easily been avoided had someone stopped them or hidden their keys.

Sydney Mickey

...

C. Joybell C.

"The only person who can pull me down is myself, and I'm not going to let myself pull me down anymore."

2

We Have God in Heaven
WHO ANSWERS OUR PRAYERS

"You are not what others think you are. You are what God knows you are." - Shannon Alder

Praise God, I am Pauline Awino Atitwa. I was born in Bunyore in Vihiga Country in Western Kenya. It was a very hard life for my parents when I was young. As with most children, I wished that my mother and father could have stayed together, but it was just too difficult for them. I was 10 years old when my parents separated.

My father was violent with my mother, and she received many beatings from him. When this would happen, my grandfather would come and take mom and us to stay with my grandfather and grandma in Mumias Matungu located in Kakamega County.

After a while, my mother made a home for me and my siblings alone, without my father in an area called Busombi Khalaba Matungu County.

It was during this time that my mom took me to school, I was 13 years old. This was the first time I had ever been in school, and I was excited to be there and to learn. When I was growing up, it was not easy for parents to get the money that was required for their children to go to school. There were school fees that had to be paid and it was very hard for my mother to get the money. She went to work in a sugar cane garden, to pay for the school fees, but the work was very hard, and my mother became ill.

There was a machine that was used in the sugar cane field, but it broke, so all the work had to be done by hand. Eventually, the company collapsed. There was no food unless we grew it in the gardens. All this work was too much for my mother and she ended up getting ammonia.

It was very difficult for my mother because she was so ill, to care for me and my siblings. My aunt asked my mom if I could go and stay with her, and my mom said," yes", so I went home with her. I was sad to leave my mom, but I had to go.

This was not a good move for me. My aunt's husband, my uncle took me to his neighbor's home and left me there. Once inside his home, the door closed, and he would not let me out. I cried all night as he would not leave me alone. When morning came, I saw the blood on the bed and knew that I was injured by what he had done to me during the night. I was so scared and sad.

I was taken to the hospital where they treated me. After my treatment, I walked the long distance back to my mother, I needed her safety and love. When my mom saw me, she started to cry because she could see that my health was not good, and she knew what I had dealt with.

Even though my mother's health was not good, and she was very sick, after a while she took me to the hospital for treatment. I was not well, and we did not know what was wrong with me. When the doctor checked me over, he said, "This young girl is pregnant." My first child was born in 1995 when I was 14 years old.

When my child turned one year old, my child's father came to my mother and asked if he could take me and our child to live with him. My mother said, "yes" because life was very hard for us, and she thought I'd have a better life with him. So off I went to live with this man, and we started a life together.

I was just 15 years old, and my husband was 18 years old when we married.

During this time, I was very sad and felt pain in my life because I missed my mom and was worried about the life she was living.

I ask my husband where his parents were because I had never met them. He told me that his mother had died when he was just three weeks old, and his father died when he was five years old. My husband was raised by his two older brothers, who were just young children themselves. My husband never had the opportunity to go to school.

In our area, when parents die, no one comes and helps. Everyone was so poor they struggled just to care for their own families. As is the custom, the children stay in the family home, but must care for themselves.

My husband and I had two more children. My second child was born when I was 16 years old and my third was when I was 19 years old. It was after the birth of my third child that I started to go to church, and I received Jesus Christ into my life.

For seven years I studied the Bible. I found enjoyment, peace, and comfort in the words that I read. I felt secure with my life.

My husband started to drink, and he started to treat me the way my father had treated my mother. It was horrible for me. Not only was my husband abusing me, but we were also very poor. My husband did not have a job that paid him a wage.

I didn't have much clothing. When it was raining, it rained inside my house and my first child became very sick. I saw the body of my child become swollen. It made me very scared, and I knew I needed to take her to the hospital.

At the hospital, the doctor said my daughter needed an operation on her joints. The hospital stay was four months and because of my husband's drinking, I decided to stay with my daughter at the hospital for all those months.

At our hospital, there was not any food for me, so my husband had to bring me food.

There is also a bill after your stay in the hospital, when you are poor it is impossible to pay. The bill at the hospital was $800.00 dollars. I had no way to pay for it. We were very poor and had no way of coming up with the money. Luckily, God sent someone to pay the bill for me.

My daughter fully healed, and I thank God that she did. This gave me faith, that I would also one day be healed. Healed of my broken heart and deep emotional wounds.

God blessed us with another child, a baby girl. I loved her so much, she was the sweetest little baby anyone could ever have.

One Sunday, I left my three-year-old daughter to play with the other children that were being cared for by another mother. When I came back from the church sermon, I found that woman had beaten my daughter. I was heartbroken. My sweet little girl, why would someone do this? She was so little.

I was told she was playing with the drinking water and dumping it off the porch. She was beaten for this. My sweet little daughter was crying because she was in so much pain.

She died that night from a broken back. I fainted when she passed and was in shock. I was devastated and became very depressed. I cried all the time and was very sad.

Nothing happened to this woman for her crime. I reported it, and there was an investigation, but there was no punishment at all. I just had to accept what had happened to my darling sweet little daughter. If you are a poor person, there is no one to stand up for you, no one would help. It was a horrible time in my life.

After some time, one Saturday, I was in the church praying to God, asking to hear words of healing. This is when I heard God speak to me. God told me to dry my tears. I was given courage and God removed the sadness in my life.

I knew that I wanted to be a Pastor and help others who needed help. My Pastor at the time removed me from the class I was in and told me it was time for me to be a leader. I was so excited and felt very proud to be able to be in the position to help others.

I became the Pastor of the Sunday School for two-year-old children. Then, I received a promotion and was promoted to be the Pastor of the youth who were three years old.

And then I became Pastor of a "home cell" group for six months. This is a group that comes together in people's homes and prays for others. And then I became a full Pastor. I was so proud of what I had done in my life and that God trusted me to help others. It was a dream for me.

I started my own church and held services under a tree for the first year. I was thinking of what I could do to get a rental house to make it a church where we could be inside, rather than outdoors.

Well, I did it! I was able to get my congregation inside rather than worshiping outside. I then decided to see if I could get the church land in a 50/50 share and God helped me to get it! Another amazing accomplishment for me.

In this church, I opened a school for children and their needs. I prayed to God that the children would be able to receive lunch. The children never had lunch as their parents were poor and could not send one. Also, some of the children had no parents, so there was no lunch for any of them. And once again God answered my prayers, and the children were able to eat at lunch hour.

I was a poor lady and relied on God to help me, my faith was strong.

Trouble soon began. There was a bishop who started fighting with me. He wanted to know how I got the plot of land for my church. He reported me to the police and then he came and took me to the police officer. He told the police that he bought everything for the church. The land, the chairs, everything!

I asked him why he would say that because it was not true. He produced papers and said that proved he paid for it all. Then he took everything, the land, the church, the equipment, everything I had worked so hard to build.

There was nothing I could do, the police believed him, a man, not me, a woman.

The police kept me in jail! They also got my husband and put him in jail with me. This meant no one was there to care for our children. They had to care for themselves. Luckily, we were only held for one week in jail. It was such a sad time for our family.

I never got my land or the chairs for the church back from him. He had everything. I decided to stop fighting and just let him keep it all. I was not getting anywhere, so I just left it alone and trusted that God would again provide all that I needed as he had done before.

Eventually, I was able to rent a house to start the church once again. Although we had the building, we had nothing else, no chairs, no benches, absolutely nothing. The church members followed me. I was so happy that I had their trust and love.

I have now had this church for seven years. We are still in need of many items but have been able to gather some seating for the church members. There are 100 members who attend the church regularly.

I hold a support group for widows, at the church, who are very poor and struggling in their lives. I do my best to direct them, encourage them, care for them, and give them the word of God. They find comfort in the word of God.

I have a Sunday school for the adults and youth members. It warms my heart to see how many come to the church.

I noticed a young girl, 13 years old, and her 2-year-old brother coming to the church. They started coming every Sunday. I spoke with them and found out that their parents had died, and the young girl was raising her little brother alone. Their life was hard, and they were not doing well. I decide to bring them home with me. I felt I could not leave them alone.

They are now part of my family. I have eight children, including my two new children from the church. There are ten people living in our home. It is hard at times, but God does give us what we need.

I have been using the Women Like Me books to teach my widows. They learn valuable life lessons from the stories of the women who bravely tell their stories. Told by women all over the world.

Women Like Me in Kenya is my dream, to help my women to tell their stories so that they can heal from their wounds and other women in the world will know about them.

God directs us and brings us together. I have no doubt of this. God can remove all your pain and sorrows if your soul inside can say "yes" and let go. If you can do this, you will forget your problems.

Pauline Atitwa

...

Jane Goodall

"What you do makes a difference, and you have to decide what kind of difference you want to make."

3

Pieces of My Heart
SEVEN MIRACLES, TWO ANGELS, AND
ONE SACRED SONG FOR LOIS

"To give visibility to love, I made a simple substitution in my most famous equation. If instead of E = mc2, we accept that the energy to heal the world can be obtained through love multiplied by the speed of light squared, we arrive at the conclusion that love is the most powerful force there is, because it has no limits."
-Albert Einstein on the Power of Love.

My mother, Lois, passed away 20 years ago. While she was transitioning over a long and difficult year, we talked a lot about Spirit, God, and what that meant to each of us.

She was in Victoria General Hospital for a very long time and wanted to be home. While we were trying to work that out, we did our best to keep her focused on the little things that brought her joy.

These included a slice of bacon here and there, the music she loved, and us just being there around the clock. She had a big window in that room, which looked out over a meadow at the back of the hospital. She loved watching the animals and birds come and go.

On one of the last mornings of her stay on Victoria, I decided to take her down to the meadow if I could. It was a spontaneous, intuitive decision not based on the reality of the task at hand.

Never the less, I managed to get her loaded onto an ambulance mobile bed and strapped in safely, as the nurses looked on with a combination of awe and anxiety as we trundled off to the elevator. We stopped briefly at the commissary to pick up drinks and ice cream and headed out of the hospital and down the hard gravel path to the meadow.

Mom was freshly bathed, blanketed, and loaded with painkillers, a Cheshire cat smile plastering her upturned face as she waved like the Queen herself to everyone we passed. It was slow yet smooth sailing down and into the meadow, fragrant with summer flowers and greenery.

Two does stepped gingerly into the meadow to graze, totally oblivious to our presence, as birds and butterflies flitted here and there. Amazingly there were no mosquitos or flies, and the squirrels were as curious about us as we them. We didn't talk much, just enjoyed the summer splendor in front of us.

When it came time to head back, I realized with a sinking heart that I had made a tactical error. I didn't factor in Mom's weight or the gravity of her bed/chariot on loose gravel going uphill. I pushed and pushed, making little to no progress, and praying all the while for someone to see our predicament from the parking lot and come to assist us.

As I muttered another prayer for help, head down and pushing hard, a young man suddenly appeared from nowhere at my side. He was in a military uniform I didn't recognize. He tipped his head giving us a mini salute as he grabbed the downhill weight. Not saying a word, he motioned me to the front to pull from there. He was taking nearly the full weight of all.

When we came adjacent to the hospital entry, another man saw us. He left his wife in a wheelchair by the doors to help us maneuver the bed through the doors to the elevator. I was concentrating on watching mom, who was laughing, in danger of falling sideways, and breathing heavily at all the excitement.

I'm sure it resembled a mini three-ring circus to all watching, especially the one gentleman's wife in the wheelchair at the side of the entrance. When we reached the elevator, I thanked him and turned to thank the kind young many only to find him gone.

He was nowhere in sight at all, I turned to the man's wife to ask her where he went, and she looked like a startled deer in headlights. I asked her where he went. She just looked at me wide-eyed, smiling broadly, and said, "POOF! He was here, and then he wasn't! Funny thing is, I could see all your reflections in the mirrors, on each side of the doors, except for his. He had no reflection, none. Yet just for a second, he was surrounded by light and then gone! I think he must have been an angel answering your prayers."

That was Angel One!

A few days later, we left Victoria. While we couldn't bring her to home, we did bring her to the hospital on Salt Spring Island, where she would be surrounded by people she knew and loved for her final journey.

I had to return to Calgary, Alberta and came for the last week of her life. That last week my sister Rene, her husband John, and I had been keeping around the clock vigil at her bedside. It was a grueling, exhausting, sorrowing time. We tried to keep it light, and loving rotating our time, playing her favorite music, and reading her favorite books aloud.

We hardly slept, and never at the same time. We took turns dozing for a few minutes at a time, one on the cot on one side of her bed and the other holding her hand from a chair on the other. As she declined rapidly, she was moved to the "family room," the one people whose days were numbered.

It was a lovely room, beautifully appointed with inspiring paintings, soft colors, and comfortable furnishings donated in appreciation by the families of previous guests. It was sad, somber, and beautiful all at the same time. Everyone knew what it meant when you went to that room.

We held her hands as we relayed the news and views of the day in town, on the island, and particularly with the "girls. " Mom, Rene, and John owned, managed, and lived in a group home with five disabled adult women, whom we all loved. They were family to us and we them. They missed mom terribly and one by one came to say goodbye in their own special way.

We rambled on with the local gossip, told racy jokes, news of her beloved grandchildren, and a newborn great-grandson. I cried buckets as I relayed his birth story to her, and we celebrated a milestone together. Rene taped a large poster-size picture of Noah, just hours old, to the ceiling of her room. It was the first and last thing she saw whenever she opened her eyes.

Other photos and artwork graced walls and tables. Photos of the beach, the garden she loved so much, the deer eating her flowers, Dad every inch the cowboy on his favorite horse, friends, parties, good times, memories to treasure always.

She was reminded of times past and especially our father. She said Dad, who had passed two decades earlier, had been to visit and sat at the end of her bed every night for a while. Her mother, who passed when she was only nine years old, came often.

Even when it was difficult and then impossible to talk, she always winked and smiled whenever she was with us to let us know she saw us. As friends came and went, Mom, drifted in and out of our reality over the final days.

She told us of visitors from the other side who also came and went throughout the days and nights. I assured her I had been there. Love, Peace, Joy, and Grace is all you will find there, in what I call the field of Infinite Unity, NOW.

Having experienced multiple near-death experiences, I discovered there are only three states of Soul being on Earth. You are either a Human BEING or a HUMAN DOING. You are either NOW HERE or NOWHERE until you choose to move to NOW IN SPIRIT, which I simply call NOW. All three exist simultaneously, like a triple-layered mirror. Those who have passed can cross back and forth as Souls IN SPIRIT.

Her doctor and a dear friend Ron, whom Mom considered a "chosen son," was in and out constantly, ensuring her pain levels were under control, checking on and comforting us. "Do whatever makes her happy!" were his parting words to us.

We sang we prayed, we laughed, cried, and did pretty much anything that came to mind that she might find meaningful and comforting. That day we had a spontaneous "Passion" party in her honor, complete with all the things she loved: Chinese food, fortune cookies, wine, and chocolate cake.

The hospital staff looked the other way as we partied throughout the day and not so decorously hooted and hollered, laughing and singing along to her favorite tunes.

She sipped wine through a straw, put food on her lips so she could taste what she could no longer swallow, and smiled widely as we basked in a little happiness.

Her fortune cookie read. "You will soon take a long and pleasant journey; however, you should expect some delays along the way"! We laugh uproariously every time we remember that to this very day.

Our brother Wayne, her only son, and his wife Pat were on their way to her and us from Alberta. They were racing furiously against holiday traffic through the Rockies, against the BC Ferry schedules to the Gulf Islands, and the Angels of Death and NOW.

When they reached the halfway mark, Wayne called to say he was almost there. Mom had not been able to speak and could barely swallow for the past 24 hours. We joked with him that it hadn't stopped her from quaffing a coffee mug of wine with a smile on her face and savoring it to the last drop.

If only we had facetime, then! We put the phone to her ear so she could hear his voice and he could talk to her once more, just in case. Her face lit up like a Christmas tree. She found her voice for just a few minutes of the last full day of her life, to tell her beloved son how much she loved him, and never spoke again.

That was MIRACLE ONE!

That night realizing the end was very near, we called her dearest friends and healers to gather in a circle with her one last time. Together we held a clearing, cleansing, healing meditation, and prayer for her and everyone who loved her.

After they left, Rene and I settled into our nightly routine. This time I was on the cot, and Rene was in a chair on the other side of the bed, holding her hand. We chatted quietly for a while, and then despite our desperate fear that she might pass, we both fell into a deep exhausted sleep.

Sometime early in the morning, I awoke with a start, my heart pounding. Something was different in the room. The energy had shifted and was palpable! The room felt fuller, denser. I could feel, yet not see, the OTHERS here NOW. Mom was gazing upward intently at nothing and everything we could not see.

I glanced at my sister asleep, leaning in towards Mom, realizing at the same time that this was it! The moment of Release at come. We had prayed so long for her not to suffer and then prayed even harder that it would not be too soon. It was happening Now Here, and Wayne was nowhere, so close and yet so far away.

Her breathing slowed and was almost gone. As I looked up from the cot, she turned her head to stare straight at me, willing me to get up. Her hand was stretched out towards me. I grabbed for it as she tried to smile and turned her gaze to my sister, and then at nothing again.

I leaped up and cried out, "Rene, wake up, it's time. She's going!" She bolted upright, nearly flinging Mom out of bed in the process. We grappled with what was happening with her, with us, and the surprise of the moment. After all, we had a plan for this. Discussed it endlessly. Like all of the best-laid plans, it wasn't perfect!

Rene cried out, "Wait for your music, Mom!" as she tried to turn on the tape player and hang onto Mom's hand at the same time. We danced a bizarre love ballet, a flashing, flailing attempt to hold her close from opposite sides of the bed, as she began her final journey.

With her favorite music, Hawaiian songs, and chants playing softly in the background.... except there was NO MUSIC.....NO CHANT-ING... AND CERTAINLY NO DRUMS... as we had so carefully, lovingly pre-planned, meticulously recorded for this specific moment.

It was becoming obvious that NOW was not going to wait for us. The tape had to be rewound and restarted! It was one of those grue-some micro-moments of panic that, in retrospect, years later, seem hysterically funny for no good reason. As if it was someone else's mother, staring wildly at us from the bed, waiting to dance into death...with no music! Damn that fortune cookie!

We heard the gasp and rattle we were dreading and desperately tried to get a grip. We held on tightly as Rene fumbled with the tape through tears, all the while screaming not so softly," No wait, Mom, don't die yet! You have to wait for your music! We planned this remember? Meanwhile, I started laughing and crying all at the same time, which made it all even more confusing.

Mom stared at us with the "look" we had known our entire life. The one she gave us when she was running out of patience and time with a situation. I am sure we looked and acted like a pair of idiot unruly children, all while she was patiently and heroically staving off the Angel of Death.

Mom did not curse unless she was really unhappy or mad. I could almost hear her in my head, "Girls, get your shit together!" She always said if a job was worth doing, it was worth doing well or not at all.

True to her word to the very end, and not wanting to distress us more than she already had, she hung on just long enough. It was the last human trick she would play on us as she went dancing, chanting, and laughing into the light.

We remained frozen, hanging onto the human shell that was no longer our mother. Speechless, we stared at each other over her body. After a long time, which was probably just a few minutes, I realized I was holding my breath. I felt unable to breathe, smothered, as cold and rigid as my mother was becoming.

Almost retching, I battled with the immediate sense of great loss and pain as waves of the familiar sterile hospital smell mingled with the stench of the room, half-drunk cups of coffee, partially eaten containers of Chinese food in the bin, and the sweet-sour smell of wine. Our encampment around her bed. Wave after wave crashed against me, waves of loss and the family memories of a lifetime.

A nurse came into the room, took Mom's vitals, confirmed there were none, closed her eyes, and went to get the doctor. I had to leave! NOW! I had to get out of that room, away from her body, to find fresh air, solace, and wait for peace in the garden. I left Rene alone in the room, waiting for John, Wayne, and Pat.

I always find myself heading on autopilot to the nearest garden in times of stress. I knew that was where my soul and my mother's soul would be waiting. I bolted headlong out the door, blinded by tears, and nearly tripped the nurse and Dr. Ron heading back in. Leaving my sister still holding Mom's hand, I clung to the door frame for support as I saw my brother coming down the hall towards me.

They knew from my face she was gone. Rene appeared beside me. All we could do was hold each other tightly. Words formed in my mind, yet I could not speak. We stared wordlessly at each other. Tears streamed down my face along with a steady clear stream of runny snot!

We held tightly to each other, letting our hearts say what our mouths could not, as Pat passed us all tissues. Stepping aside finally, I laughed ruefully and said, " Where energy goes, fluid flows, something I have always known to be true."

They moved into the room, and we left them to have time alone with her as Rene went with Dr. Ron to make the necessary arrangements. We knew our brother was heart-broken to have just missed being together at the end of our journey with her and needed time with her to process.

I continued on resolutely towards the door at the end of the hall. Beyond it lay a small beautiful patio peace garden overlooking the edge of the town of Ganges. Light was pouring through the window, inviting me into the garden. I took a seat in the sunlight at a small wrought iron table to slowly absorb the immediate crippling pain of my mother's passing.

I heard it again, in both my mind and heart, the Hawaiian chants speeding her onwards to the light. Something felt very familiar about that. I was praying to anything and everything listening that she was speeding to the light, with my father, her parents, her stepbrother, and all the others. To the Love of All that IS.

I saw her standing with them in a blaze of heavenly colors. I asked that Love ease our pain and loss as I called to all my Angels for guidance and a sign. My consciousness was so focused in the heart, so distant from the here and now.

Something made me look up and out across the valley below and slowly skyward. I saw a speck of soft shining white high above me circling gently down toward me. At first, I thought it was a leaf, a feather, or a bit of paper and glanced away.

I did not see or feel the butterfly as she dropped lower and lower and then settled gently, purposely upon my knee. The scent of nearby gardenias and roses, two of Mom's favorite flowers, filled the air and drew my attention to them. I glanced down and was transfixed. She was so fragile, so beautiful, so immediate, so NOW!

She radiated colors of creation, passion, peace, and tranquility. Her wings glowed softly pearl-like burnished shades of yellow, orange, red, and white, finely edged in black. They quivered delicately as she patiently waited to connect. As small as she was, I felt cradled in her delicate and loving wings, held in my mother's love. The loss left, and only peace remained. We were one together in NOW.

She stayed with me in the garden the entire time, dancing above my head, flitting from arm to shoulder to arm to thigh to hand as I waited for my family to join us there.

I heard the door open again, and my family stepped into the light. I turned my head towards them, tears of joy in my eyes, smiling broadly. Everyone was silent, stunned, and mesmerized at the same time. The confirmation of all we had discussed was NOW HERE, in our reality from another dimension.

Mom had said many times over the previous years of suffering that, if she could, when she transitioned, she would send us each a sign in our own time and place of peace. Mine would be a butterfly, Rene's would be an angel or angelic symbol, and Wayne's would be an eagle.

It was one of the most sacred moments in my life. Before this beautiful spirit left, she rose high, circling above us in a perfect figure eight. To me, that represented a symbol of Infinite Unity.

I knew with my whole being that this was the spirit of my mother letting us know she was peacefully, joyously released from Earth, reunited with Source, and on her way to a higher vibration and state of BEING. Shortly after that, both my siblings received their signs from her that she was safe on the other side.

Since that time, whenever I am struggling with anything in my life, in need of inspiration, confirmation, or release in any way, a butterfly appears in one way or another. Even in the depth of winter or where none are known to be. When that happens, the joy I feel is indescribable.

That was MIRACLE TWO

Six months later, we returned her ashes to her true heart home, the north shore of the Hawaiian Island of Oahu, and briefly into the arms of her second partner, Bambi, the last and deepest love of her life. He was her one true Soul Mate, a gentle Hawaiian giant who transitioned and joined her not long after.

When we arrived to meet him, he was waiting at the pier with his son, Kelii, and a small group of elder women dressed in beautiful Mumu's with white, yellow, and red flowers in their hair and leis around their necks, along with one lone drummer carrying a boom box.

Each of us girls was wearing one of Mom's favorite Mumu's as we stood on the pier with them. Mom's ashes were in an urn cradled lovingly in Bambi's arms. The elders began chanting along with the recording of the very song we had played at her passing.

They formed a circle around us and led us forward in a circle of musical prayer as we boarded the boat. Bambi handed the urn to my brother and remained on the pier, the leader of a Circle of Love, singing us out to sea.

They were there to assist Bambi in carrying her back to the Sacred Mother Earth in song as we consecrated her remains to the crystal-clear ocean. She always wanted to be here and continue to travel! The chant continued, reverberating far out over the water, following us to our destination.

I didn't immediately notice the beautiful butterfly following us down the pier and gently landing and settling in the back of the boat until my sister pointed to her. A fair distance out, we stopped and talked with Mom, sharing some of our favorite memories.

The ocean was calm, rocking us gently as we each cast some of her ashes out along with a red hibiscus bloom for John's mother, symbolically reuniting them as there as the great friends they were in life.

We also tossed a beautiful lei shining brightly in the ocean and the heart home she cherished and had missed for so long, uniting all our families as one. We watched as her earthly remains floated nearby, mixing with the vivid turquoise waters.

Slight foaming waves overlapped each other, yet not the beautiful glowing lei as it ever so gently formed a heart around her slowly sinking ashes. Its fragrant scent intensified as it cradled her soul, final and free. We held a collective breath as this ballet of love danced before us on the waves in an unbelievable circle around the boat, thus encircling us as well.

Seemingly from nowhere, the forgotten butterfly appeared, flying higher and higher into the air circling the boat several times. We watched until it disappeared from sight and then looked back at the lei as it continued circling the boat against the current and incoming tide until all the ashes sank out of sight. Then it too began sinking into the mother waters with our mother.

That was Miracle Three

Kekii said he wanted to show us one of Mom's favorite places. We headed further out to sea. He told us about a hidden gem. It was a sandbar that appeared suddenly from nowhere.

At first, from a distance, you couldn't see the sandbar. We could see people playing and sitting there. Water washed over it, and from that distance, it looked like the people were floating on lawn chairs.

As he navigated towards it, he told us many things we did not know about his family, himself, and what our mother meant to them. Then he turned to me, pointed down to the water, and said, "I dreamed about this last night. I told Dad about it."

He leaned towards me, grinning broadly, and pointing down beside the boat, "Your Hawaiian spirit has come to greet you." Waving towards the sandbar and slowing the boat to a near stop, he continued, "We will meet you later."

I looked down to the sea in questioning wonder. Beside the slow-moving boat, swimming directly beside me was a huge green sea turtle. Without thinking, I threw off my Mumu and dove over the side and deep into the cool water, the deepest free dive I had ever done.

Knifing down through the crystalline water, part of me wondered how he knew I would do that and slowed the boat just enough. Just an arm's length away, she followed me.

The peace and perfection of the moment was mesmerizing, spontaneous, and as old as mankind. I felt at one with the sea, my mother, and the ancient seer swimming beside me, and all that is.

It felt so natural, as if I had always been a part of this other world. I forgot I wasn't breathing, couldn't breathe, and dove further yet. Too far...I knew it.. yet part of me was unwilling to return, willing me further, begging me to stay. I wanted it! I felt so free.

My beautiful Spirit Guide followed me down, farther, and farther. Then in a flash, she was under me and guiding me upwards, swimming me back to the light, to the surface and life. We swam up gently, slowly, eye to eye, shoulder to shell, soul to soul, NOW ONE with Creator together.

We honored the great wisdom we shared together on this brief journey as she guided me back to myself and land. I never once felt without air, strained against the tide, or was fearful of drowning. I knew we were divinely protected as she swam me all the way to the sandbar in the middle of the deep blue bay.

I knew then, as she looked deeply into my eyes one last time, turned away, and swam out of sight. I knew at that moment that I would never allow myself to sink again in life. I acknowledged that I had been living in the past, mired in pain, fear, and heartbreaking memories that were drowning me as surely as the ocean was now releasing me.

And then I KNEW...the universal journey of life was just one long deep dive after another. Just when you thought you could not breathe again....you did not want to breathe again...you would not come back, NOW HERE called, guiding you back to exactly where you needed to be to claim and take the next steps forward.

You, me, we, are called back again and again, through our individual experiences and challenges, until we finish what we have divinely chosen to come here to do. We are not released until our mission is complete.

Life is hitting the surface, gasping for breath, for life! You live it! NOW! You breathe it! Coming back to the surface is the meaning of life. Despite all its difficulties, twists, turns, detours, as well as the love and joy we create and find along the way. It simply IS until it ISN'T, and then it IS again NOW when you return. It is your CHOICE!

I chose to live fully engaged in my life again, regardless of what showed up to deter or detour me along the way. Life had new meaning for me. I knew that even though I didn't yet have a clue what that meant going forward, I would keep choosing LIFE.

That was Miracle Four!

When we returned to shore, I wandered into a small shop on the pier. One of the grandmothers who had sung for us worked out in the shop. I told her I wanted to buy a sarong. She gave me a hug and handed me a sarong she thought would be perfect for me and help me remember this day always. I opened it to see a beautiful pearly butterfly imprinted on a sea of red, orange, yellow, and white.

That was Miracle Five!

A few days later, with permission and a trusted native guide, we set out on a journey from the seashore and up a mountainside to an ancient sacred waterfall. We were not allowed to carry cameras to the falls. We felt blessed and honored just to be allowed to go there and pray for the spiritual journey of our mother. It was a glorious day, clear, blue, fragrant, and peaceful.

We barely talked as we hiked halfway up the mountain, awed by the silence, the birdsong, and the twists and turns in the trail. It was steep and challenging, with new vistas around every turn. When we came upon the falls, they tumbled halfway down the mountainside, dazzling, shooting rainbows through the mists, gloriously backlit by palms and dense vegetation.

The pool at the bottom was cool and deep indigo blue. Birds and butterflies were everywhere. I cannot remember the name now, just that I called it: Mother Earth's Temple at the time. We moved apart as we came to the sacred pool. Wayne and Pat held hands and walked to the other side of the glen and pool as Rene, Linda, and I stood a little bit apart and gazed in awe upwards, our hearts joined in silent prayer.

As we watched the waterfall spewing out rainbows, the mist deepened on a shaded ledge about halfway up the falls to our right. As the sunlight slowly crept towards it, what looked like the outline of a woman took shape and then turned into what appeared to be an Angel!

The rainbows around it glistened in jewel-like colors, and the mists swirled as the breeze picked up. We looked on with amazement as we felt overwhelming love and confirmation that our journey was complete.

The angel was there a few minutes and then just disappeared into the mist. We never said a word, just looked at each other, smiling with joy and filled to the brim with hope and joy and grace. If my brother saw it, he has never said. My sister and I have talked of it often, and what a confirmation it was to both of us.

That was When Angel Two Appeared

I returned from that journey filled with hope, a new sense of me, and a confirmation of Now, of miracles big and small all around me, and that more were on the way. My whole being was re-charged and vibrating with energy I thought I would never feel again.

As a result, my life choices changed dramatically, and a new map of my future and universe began to take shape. As I began to imagine and confirm a different view of my reality, my reality changed to mirror those choices. The journey I began to reunite my mother with her sacred space became the journey back into me, away from what was safe and familiar territory.

I was changed, yet the same, new, and yet as old as the universe. Resistance, fear of the unknown, and of making another mistake in my life died. New patterns of being, breathing, and living emerged, and I embraced them.

Around each corner, a new teacher appeared, and I listened. I could hear their drums, hear their songs, and yet not read their music.

Most of it felt familiar yet sometimes made no sense to me at the time. A lot of it was simply white noise, spiritual elevator music. I had to learn again how to trust my intuition and my heart to set new higher energy intentions from this renewed compass and passion for life.

Shortly after my mother's death, I reunited with my partner of the previous six years. It was a fair yet futile attempt to band-aid a relationship that would never have happened, let alone continue, if I had trusted myself.

It was born from loneliness, shame, blame, guilt, and fear, fanned by the simple fact that we made decent roommates who didn't demand or expect too much of each other. We lived a life of comfort alone together, something I had learned previously to be very good at.

We had parted briefly, twice before Mom's illness, then tried again on his terms after her death. He had convinced me that all of our time together had been on my terms, where I worked and lived. He had come to me.

We should give it our best shot based on his choices, his employment, and taking the helm as captain of the ship we called love. It seemed fair at the time, and if it didn't work, well, I would have at least tried and been fair. We were always very good at living in Chaos and Incoherence.

It didn't work simply because it was never supposed to. We had just become accustomed to living in chaos and incoherence, cleverly disguised as our comfort zone. We parted and remained friends. Neither of us wanted to inflict more pain or hurt each other more than we already had. I knew I didn't love him and perhaps never had.

We were simply roommates with privileges. We were never meant to be anything more than a way station for each other on the way to something, somewhere, or someone else. We had detoured on our path together for a while to lick our wounds and find companionship and comfort until we had the courage to find our true paths.

After returning from Hawaii, I knew I couldn't accept or live as I had or was anymore. I checked my heart compass and resolved to leave him for good. He was on a road I could not and would not travel on.

I saw clearly what I knew to be true and couldn't face before. I knew from the beginning of the relationship, breakups, and reunions that it was nothing more than comfortable for both of us. True passion and peace did not exist in it.

What did exist was simply conditioning from our previous lives and a recipe for failure. Or was it? I knew to find peace, I had to find value in it rather than judgment of it. Only then would I adjust my compass and trust my true self again.

The universe had moved me, taught me a lesson I had refused to learn in earlier relationships, and everything I once defined as failed. I was not going to do that again. I trusted my intuition and my heart compass in a way I hadn't since early childhood.

I moved on and out, this time without the habitual fear of the unknown and starting all over again. It wasn't easy. It was doable, and I did it. Along the way, I found peace and more. In fact, I felt calm, centered, excited, and even perhaps even what might be described as truly happy with myself for the first time in a decade.

I did not worry or fear my future. My father would have said, I didn't have a pot to piss in or a window to throw it out of. It simply didn't matter to me. I found the gift in this parting, as painful and grown-up as it was, was the unwavering faith that I was held in the arms of NOW, and this was all meant to be.

My soul was stretching, flying, diving, growing wildly, and reaching farther than it had ever gone before. My eyes and heart were wide open. I no longer fit in the old shoes I called my life and went shopping. For the first time in my life, I was choosing based just on me.

I didn't need or want counsel or support from anything, or anyone, except my family, my Angels, and God. I was beginning to remember, renew, and regain the broken bits of my soul.

I did not need to be partnered to feel secure or validated. I did not need or want anyone to take care of me. I did not care what anyone felt or thought about what I should do or where I should go. BEING rather than DOING was validation enough!

That was Miracle Six

This journey was my choice and my purpose. It would unfold according to NOW. If I remained in NOW, connected to all that is, everything would unfold accordingly, how it was meant to be, when it was meant to be, where it was meant to be in my divine dance with Infinite Unity. God laughed, and my Angels danced!

Before I could even grasp what was happening, I had a new job, a new home, and a totally new life opened up for me like magic. Because I wasn't looking new man entered my life.

Together we would create the space for untold miracles. Together we joined a drum circle, make, and paint a drum together, where I wrote a drum song honoring my mother and our journey together. The rest is another chapter for another book. Until then, I hope you enjoy the song.

That was Miracle Seven!

This Chapter and the Song that follows are dedicated to my mother, Clara "Lois" Deschamps.

Her favorite saying: "Do it right the first time or pay the price later."

Her favorite quote:

The purpose of life is to live it, to taste experience to the utmost, to reach out eagerly, and without fear, for newer and richer experience
- Eleanor Roosevelt

Sacred Heart Mother Drum Song
Let your heart be still, now
Listen, hear her sweet song, now
Breathe from her heart, now
Soar now and Sing, now

Dance, now, dance
The song of the Sacred Mother now
Heartbeat of Life, now
Sacred Heart Mother Drum now

The butterfly whirls, as the Mother dances
The sea sounds her sirens call, now
To the shores of our hearts, now
Once so far, far, apart,

Reunited, now, mysterious now,
Magical, now,
Our mythical stars shining, now
Swirling now, whirling now

Our universe turning, now
The drum sings softly now
Loudly now, far away now
Our songs overlap, now

Over and over now,
moving closer and closer now
Now here, now there, everywhere now
The butterfly whirls, so softly she sparkles

As once we were, are now,
and ever shall be, now
Sacred Mother Heart still hears now!
She breathes, in Spirit now!

The drum beats her heart, now!
Sacred heart songs, from the soul, now!
Sung from heart to heart, now!
Dear heart is as it ever was now

Ever shall BE NOW!

My journey continues with Purpose in Love and Light.

May it also be true for you.

Namaste

Donna Fairhurst

...

J.K. Rowling

"Understanding is the first step to acceptance, and only
with acceptance can there be recovery."

4

A Child of a Survivor of a Residential School
DO WHAT YOU LOVE, LOVE WHAT YOU DO

"Today I know my identity, who I am, where I come from. This little girl has been reborn, to love herself, and respect herself. I can now look in the mirror and love what I see. Let go, Let God."
- Tania Dashcavich

Well, where do I start? A little about my roots. I am a child of a survivor of residential schools. My mother, Janet, was born at Jackfish Lake on reserve under Athabasca Chipewyan First Nation Treaty 8 Territory.

She was taken away from her home and family and placed into Holy Angels Residential School, Fort Chip, Alberta, in Canada. While there, she developed tuberculosis and was sent to Charles Camsell Hospital in Edmonton.

When she got better, the authorities placed her into foster care. She never got to come home to Fort Chipewyan and her family.

My mom met my dad, who is Ukrainian, when she was of legal age to marry. They were so in love. After marrying, they had my brother and me. We had the greatest upbringing! We went camping a lot, and it was so much fun.

Dad was a hard-working man, and he supported his family well. We had a beautiful home in the city. Mom taught us the values we needed to know and gave us both plenty of love. We had everything we needed during that time of my life.

This was until my dad got sick in 1982 with cancer. I didn't know how bad it was until two years later when he passed away. And then my journey of trauma from loss and grief started.

After his passing, my mother began to drink. We then moved from place to place; our life was no longer stable within the city. I had to take care of myself, and I learned to survive.

When I met my first child's father, I thought he was the one! I was crazy about him. At the time, I didn't realize I was looking for that father figure I had longed for since losing my father.

I stayed six years in that relationship. We tried everything to stay together. We even went for treatment because of our addictions. However, my firstborn child was born, and he didn't stay long. Our relationship was unhealthy, so we separated. It was another feeling of loss and grief trauma for me.

Well, it didn't take me long, and I was in another relationship. By this time, I was drinking, and smoking weed and was unhealthy. I was neglecting my mother duties. Thankfully for my mother, she helped me with my kids during their upbringing.

So here I was in another unhealthy relationship. I got sober again and went into a treatment center for my addiction. Then I became pregnant, and I had my second born. I was thinking I was going to have this beautiful family, but it was not to be. Once again, I was looking for this father figure, but of course, it wasn't happening. My boyfriend wanted to separate, and I found I was on my own with two kids, with two different dads! A single mama!

During this time, I was drinking again, neglecting my kids' and mother's duties. Here I am again alone, a single mom suffering from loss and grief trauma for the third time. It was a hard time in my life.

Then I met my third daughter and son's dad. I was repeating the same lifestyle, but I didn't see it. I never got it! I just kept drinking and drugging and, sadly, neglecting my kids. I was leaving my oldest to watch the others and take on my mother duties.

This relationship didn't work out either. Abuse was all I knew. I lived with grief and loss from my dad's death and my childhood home. I was so hurt. This is where the cycle continued, trauma, grief, and loss.

I was suicidal, and full-on depression had set in. I was just here, just existing, completely numb. I didn't know that I had Post Traumatic Stress Disorder, depression, anxiety, addictions, and was suffering from mental, physical, spiritual, and emotional abuse. I was a mess.

After having four kids and being a single mom, I felt I failed in so many ways. Not knowing there were unresolved issues buried in my hurts, my grief, my losses, and bringing it on to my kids. I had put the responsibility onto my oldest girl. She lost her childhood because of me. My daughter, my son's sister, was more of a mother figure than me because of my selfish ways and my addictions. Sure, I was there physically, but not mentally, spiritually, and emotionally. This is where their sister came in.

By this time, I was actively into addictions, drinking every second day, every weekend, on special occasions, any excuse I could find to drink. I wanted to feel good, to feel happy, so in my mind, this is how I was coping, burying my hurt feelings. I had no respect for myself and hated myself, from my looks to everything about me.

This went on until my first grandbaby was born. I remember I was hungover, helping my teen daughter in the delivery room. I was so sick. But when I saw her being born, a love came over me right there, and then I knew things were going to change!

My daughter was a teen mother at the time, not knowing her daughter would save me. Seeing my grandbaby come into this world, I cried. The love was totally different for my grandbaby.

I didn't quit drinking right away. But six months later, I did! I will never forget it. I was drinking for two days straight. It was my daughter's 18th birthday, and I was drinking with her. I thought it was okay, when really noooo!

I was so hungover and sick that my heart was racing. I was so scared I went into the nursing station. M sugar was 13. My blood pressure was 180 over 90! I was asked what I was doing, and I told them honestly. They told me no more drinking and to come back in a week. They told me they would check me again. They gave me my meds and sent me on my way.

That week was scary! I went back in, and sure enough, they said because I was a gestational diabetic with all four pregnancies', my drinking and not dealing with my healing which was needed, today I am a diabetic. I have high blood pressure and high cholesterol; it was a wake-up call. The doctor said I could live, or I could die. I thought of my grandbaby. I needed to be here for her, watch her grow to be a positive example for her.

So right there and then, I quit drinking, sugar, and salt, changed my lifestyle lost 60 pounds. I was eating healthy and walking. It was tough. I was in a small community. But this time around, I did it for me! I never went to a treatment center. The resources were all here. I just had to look for them. I wanted it so badly that I worked hard for it.

I cried. I believe that every tear was healing. I shared and got it all out so someday there won't be tears, and it's easier to speak. The first year I started up Alcoholics Anonymous from my home, it was like God guided me along the way. I was grateful for my mother's support, cousins, and friends I met on the way, so thankful for all of them.

It was tough at times because my mother was in the room when I shared, but she understood and never got mad. I helped her because now she was coming with me to workshops. Mom shared her story as well. One thing I will never forget was when she said she was going to die, not telling her story of the residential school. She had not even told us, her kids. But now she did, and we healed together.

I knew why my mother did what she did. She lost her identity. Who was she? She lost her language and her siblings. When my dad died, we were all lost in grief trauma. We lost our identity. Who were we?

My mother and my relationship grew. In our relationship, we became the best of friends! She said she was sorry, and I said mine. We got sober together, and mom and I healed together. Today I know how important it was to get the word SORRY out. That was the day I moved on.

Let go, let God. Now I've found my spirituality and my God. Mentally I found what works for me. I smudge, pray, and I read the bible scriptures. I do what works for me because we are all different; not everyone has the same beliefs. We must be mindful and respectful of others. I pray every day, all day. I will never take anything personally because I know it has nothing to do with me. Empathy and compassion are key to accepting people, places, and things.

I have a different mindset, but it took years of work, healing, dealing with acceptance, letting go, letting God, taking training workshops, and understanding I have a mental illness. It's okay, loving myself and accepting my past so I can move on with my future.

Twelve years of sobriety is a big accomplishment for me. As a mixed blood part Dene, Cree, and Ukrainian, finding my roots on both sides of my parents. Their history. Where do they come from, and where do I come from? Who am I? I know today both sides. They were hard workers who suffered a lot on both nationalities, my families, on both sides.

I now know my identity. Walking a sober road helped me see and feel with a different heart. I lost a lot, but today I am learning my language. I drum. I sing. I make Cabbage rolls and use my Babas good dishes on special occasions. It's the little things that matter. Even if I learn a word in dene Cree, Ukrainian or make a traditional dish, like cabbage rolls, perogies, fry moose meat, make Bannock or do a beading project, smudge pray, I have connected in away where I feel the pride of who I am and where I come from. Finding my identity, I do believe, plays a big part in our lives.

Change only comes from us doing the work. When the time is right, you will know, and God creator, will bring you to it so you can heal and deal with your issues and move on. I believe we all hit a point in our life where we've had enough, and we want better. God creator will guide us. He knows when the time is right.

Today I work at the school. I work with youth families. I earned many certificates and completed many training and healing workshops. I cried. I felt and healed this heart of mine. I mended it once again. Sometimes it is tough to not forget, but then I know why I remembered, it's to heal.

I believe this child of a survivor of residential school is making a change using my voice, practicing my traditions, and practicing my language because this generation we can help. I am proud of my mother. She may be gone physically but lives on in spirit and within me, my children's grandchildren. Her legacy lives on, and I know she has been guiding us all along our way.

———

Today I know my identity, who I am, and where I come from. This little girl has been reborn to love herself and respect herself. I can now look in the mirror and love what I see.

Let go, let God.

Tania Dashcavich

...

Sharon Salzberg

"You yourself, as much as anybody in the entire universe, deserve
your love and affection."

5

Why Every Child Should Matter

ANOTHER STORY OF OUR SHATTERED CHILD WELFARE SYSTEM.

"It is easier to build up a child than to repair an adult"
- Dr. Joe Dispenza

I said "Goodbye," and then I hung up the phone. It took all my control to hold back the angry tears that had been drowning me for weeks. The words I had just heard were so disgusting, and even worse, they had come from a social worker.

A couple of weeks before that phone call, I had gone to court to say goodbye to all the hopes and dreams I had for a child who had called me "Mommy" for almost seven years. Danica was my first foster child and was only to stay for three months. Three months turned to six...and then three years. By this time, the Ministry of Children and Families (MCFD) had given me the choice of adopting her, or they would look for a 'Forever Family.' I jumped at the chance to legally bind this child to me, as she had been in my heart from day one.

The fact that Danica had been part of my family for three years and that I had a Home Study done just weeks before her placement didn't matter. I had to undergo a second home study. I like to call it a "make-work" project. But as any Foster parent knows, you jump through the hoops no matter how ridiculous, so I did. That process took about two years. By the time I was nearing completion, a new social worker was coming on board. As soon as she came on board, she single handily changed the care plan. I went from signing the papers for an open adoption to facing the fact I might never see the child of my heart again.

A year passed, and then came November 5, 2003. The birth Mom had filed to have the Continuing Care Order (CCO) struck down. MCFD was not opposing, and I knew the outcome before I dropped my heart child off at kindergarten and entered the courtroom with family and friends at my side.

I had to be there. I knew I was not allowed to speak to the Judge, but I wanted her to know that we were devastated by the loss of this child. As I stood beside my parents and daughters, with my support 'family' behind me, the Judge prepared to make her ruling. Before she did so, she asked me directly who we were and why we were in the courtroom. My heart was pounding in my ears. I answered, 'We are her Foster Family" Her Honor looked a bit taken aback. She kindly said, "You understand you can't have a voice in this court?" to which I replied, 'We have never had a voice."

Her Honor questioned the MCFD legal counsel, asking for an explanation as to why it took seven years for the proceeding now before her. There was no clear answer. The Judge chastised the Ministry workers for their handling of the whole situation. Why had the child and the others involved been put through such a process? And why was there not a 'Supervision Order' requested to ensure a smooth transition for the child? The Social worker could only shrug and say that she was sure that all the adults involved would "continue to act like adults" (whatever legal meaning that has).

Her Honor then made her ruling. I remember hearing words, not sentences. "As MCFD did not oppose...I have grave reservations...two families here today...King Solomon...the child shall be returned to the birth parent" Through my own tears, I looked up at Her Honor, who also had tears in her eyes. I thought I was imagining that until I looked at the Bailiff and watched her wipe her tears.

Three days after the birth parent had been granted custody, she threw the "good faith agreement" in the toilet. She decided that the transition was too drawn out and cut the "access" time in half. I was beside myself. No matter what pain I was feeling, my thoughts kept going to Danica and wondering what she would be feeling. How confusing was it for her to be suddenly taken from her friends, her school, her pets...her family?

And to be honest, my family was not fairing well with the loss. My husband fell into depression. My other foster children were wondering what their futures held, and my own daughters were angry with the Ministry for taking their little sister. My whole family was grieving, and nobody understood—especially the Social Worker.

I had contacted the social worker to explain the change in the "good faith agreement" and was told that there was nothing the Ministry could do. It was out of their hands because there was no supervision order. The birth parent had the sole right to allow or not allow contact with us. The worker also tried to put the blame on me by commenting that I had been "too emotional" throughout the process" and the mother was simply reacting to that. When I raised my concerns about how Danica must be re-acting to the situation and all of the trauma it had to be causing, my comments were 'poo-pooed.' The worker said Danica had to "get used to her mother's way of handling things." She was, after all, the parent now.

I was grateful for the shock that enveloped me over the following weeks. That is what got me through dealing with my loss and that of my family. But the shock soon turned to anger when the next phone call came. The worker had called because the birth parent had complained about all the items I had sent with Danica when she left our home. Some of the clothing no longer fit, and some of the toys were no longer 'age appropriate". I explained that it was impossible for me to go through each piece of clothing and the toys were stuffed animals that Danica had been attached to and had for comfort. I also explained how difficult the situation had been for one of my children. Then came the final blow. The worker said, "Well, maybe it's time your children learn what Fostering is all about."

The Mama bear in me blew! The response started with "How dare you!" and ended with me hanging up. I knew that the way I handled that conversation would end up with me having some unsavory comments added to my fostering file. But frankly, I didn't give a crap.

So, with no support from the Ministry, I carried on. I cherished each and every moment I was given with Danica. Unfortunately, they got fewer and fewer. Danica's birth parent kept cutting and changing the visits. I grew more and more frustrated. Though part of my desire to see Danica was completely selfish, I was trying to act in Danica's best interest. I had sat through how many Ministry sponsored classes on Attachment Disorder. How many times had I been told what horrors could be visited upon a child due to lack of stability? And what if the birth parent could not parent Danica? This had been the issue in the past. I was not convinced that the move had been in Danica's best interest but rather in her birth parents. There had been numerous tries in the past to send Danica back to her. Each time she would sabotage the situation. Why would it work now?

So, I began looking into filing a court order under the "persons with significant ties" clause. This would put the court back in charge and ensure a proper transition and was something, as the Judge pointed out, the Ministry should have done. This action was met with the threat of closing down my foster home, which was a typical move made by social workers when a foster parent dared to question them. That was about the time that the fight in me gave up. I had to accept the fact that I had lost a child.

I went through the motions of living for months. People would say, "you seem to be handling things quite well," and from the outside, that's what it looked like. But inside, I was literally aching for the child that I had lost. I cried in my bathtub every single night for a year. Every single night. I hid it from my family as I didn't feel it made sense to burden them. I turned to my foster parent friends, and their support was amazing. They understood every feeling I was having when it seemed that no one else on the planet could fathom what I was experiencing. They were my saviors.

A year after the loss of Danica, I looked up from the frozen foods section in the grocery store and came face to face with the woman who had ripped out my heart one short year before...Danica's birth mom. And as quickly as I saw her, I saw Danica beside her. The chill that came over me had nothing to do with the grocery aisle I was standing in. For a moment, I froze. And then, in slow motion, I watched Danica's mom speak to her and point in my direction. As Danica looked up and met my eyes, her face broke into the most beautiful smile I had ever seen. As she ran towards me with open arms, I knew this moment would be a turning point. I didn't know how, but I knew.

It took another grocery store run in a couple of years later, but Danica's mom reached out to me on Facebook, and we talked a great deal about how we had each handled the situation at first. Apologies were made, and healing began between the two moms who loved the same child. We also agreed that the social workers had failed all of us. She did not give us the support and respect we deserved, and she caused trauma to an innocent child, a child who deserved better than being treated like a puppy who was transitioned to a new home. We also found a place to heal in a very unusual relationship, without the interference of people who could never understand what we had endured.

As the years went by, Danica also reached out to me. Having her back in my life has been a gift that I will be forever grateful for, but that's a whole other chapter to be written.

Some may think that all the healing would have brought this chapter of my life to a happy ending, but unfortunately, I don't feel that way. How can I sit back when I know about the thousands of children and families who have suffered the same fate? Our Foster care system is in shatters. Nothing will change until stories like this are shared, and society begins to understand that these children, who are discarded by their birth parents and then again by the government, deserve the same love and compassion that we give to all the children who are lucky enough to have stable homes.

We are being bombarded in the media by stories of past traumas suffered by aboriginal families. Traumas that began decades ago. We are being encouraged as a society to use compassion and under-standing. To listen and learn from how innocent children were traumatized in the past. Yet very little has changed from a political and bureaucratic standpoint for any of the children in care today, aboriginal, or otherwise.

Some people feel the situation is hopeless, and others are fine with the status quo. Most folks I know have no idea of how the failures of our child welfare system affects each and every one of us in some manner or another. Children who grow up in care are fifty percent more likely to become involved in substance abuse, teen pregnancy, crime, have mental health issues, attachment disorders, homeless-ness...the list goes on. They are also less likely to graduate or have the opportunity for post-secondary education. If people can't see how this affects them directly, well, frankly, I feel sorry for them. Living with such a lack of compassion must be miserable for them.

Every day, I plant a little seed of hope. Sometimes it comes in the form of showing compassion to a child in need, and sometimes it comes out as a rant at a social worker or politician. I do this for all the other Danica's out there who have been thrown to the wolves by those who were supposed to protect them. I believe that nothing will change until we learn that every child truly matters, and I hope I live to see the day.

Brenda-Lee Huot-Hunter

...

Susan Sontag

"Do stuff. Be clenched, curious. Not waiting for inspiration's shove or society's kiss on your forehead. Pay attention. It's all about paying attention. Attention is vitality. It connects you with others. It makes you eager. Stay eager."

6

Denying the Power of Grief
RUNNING FROM THE PAIN OF SADNESS

"It's an honor to be in grief. It's an honor to feel that much, to have loved that much." - Elizabeth Gilbert"

Our life experiences are based on dates. The significance of these dates shapes who we are and how we lead our lives. These writings are my journey through the significant dates in my life. They are being written to express my truth of who I am and how I have behaved navigating through these significant dates.

Many of us have felt true happiness and great sadness in our lives. Many greater than others. How do we learn how to cope with sadness?

August 7, 2012

Ten years ago, I felt the deep darkness of losing one of the most important people in my life, my mom. At age 66, she was gone. My mom had a huge heart, and if you were lucky enough to cross her path, she met you with unconditional love. She touched many with her kindness and had an infectious giggle that would set the room off. She was not shy to voice her opinion whether you asked for it or not, yet she was your confidant when you most needed it. My mom would drop off treats at the school where I worked. Everyone loved her thoughtfulness. She was thoughtful, alright, but it was also a reminder that I hadn't touched base for a few days. Oh yes, Mom – I miss you!

My mom battled uterine cancer. However, five years later, the cancer was back with a vengeance. Before her cancer barged back into her life, she was fearful, which was read in her face daily. However, once her diagnosis was confirmed, she was as calm as she could be and tried to embrace this devastating pain she was about to endure. As everyone would agree, to see a loved one in pain and knowing the end was catching up with her was mentally taxing, and our hearts were broken.

Once she was admitted to palliative care, we alternated days and nights. She needed to see the name on the board to know who was going on shift to be her partner in crime. There came a day when her pain was so overwhelming that the doctors prescribed inducing a comma for her final days. Such a surreal meeting to have in a hospital room, participating in a conversation that was going to neutralize your mom.

At this stage, my dad was not comfortable having visitors at the hospital. He wanted everyone to remember her vibrant character and not her physical decline. Going to the hospital for the next few weeks was our daily activity – a Deja Vu. It was lonely. The cafeteria in the Abbotsford Hospital makes the best egg sandwich - absolute comfort food. My family just adjusted to me going to the hospital every day. My sisters, dad, and aunt were squatters in the room as she was never alone.

The night she passed, we all decided to go for dinner together. It was like she needed a peaceful moment from all of us to prepare herself. My dad and aunt returned from dinner to have her leave us a couple of hours later. When my dad called, it was weird. I blurted, "She died!" Complete denial that she was gone.

We held a beautiful service for her to a large crowd – standing room only on the balcony. It was challenging to receive her guests, and many were not greeted with a warm embrace as it was an out-of-body experience.

Now what? Adjusting to a different routine, which does not involve going to the hospital. Having to introduce yourself back into your world, which didn't stop even though you feel like yelling from the roof top that your mom just died. I was lost and beginning to spiral into denial of what had happened and how was I going to deal with it.

I was currently on an anti-depressant for a few years to combat perimenopause. I went to the West Coast Women's Clinic and a natural path but with my mom being ill and having three busy children, neither recommended discontinuing the prescription.

I remember saying to my doctor, "It's just the circle of life." My doctor said, "No – your mother just died" however, I was doing whatever I could to convince myself I was not suffering.

I have always been a social bunny enjoying evenings of wine and good food. I went through the motions of work and running my household. I thought my immediate loved ones were well looked after. Yes, they had the necessities but what they were missing beyond those daily interactions was the whole me.

May 25, 2015

Six months after my mom passed, my dad was diagnosed with leukemia. The emergency doctor said he had six to nine months to live. Are you kidding me? It was beyond believable. Immediately, he was sent by ambulance to the leukemia center at Vancouver General

Hospital (VGH). He was very lucky to have a bed on the ward as he was 69 years of age, and this particular ward only holds 26 beds and focuses on younger patients.

We were very grateful his journey lasted two years versus the six to nine months originally diagnosed. The VGH ward was intense. We wore gloves, gowns, and masks. His stay was brief, and then he became an outpatient for blood transfusions. My dad loved to shop and was quite the fashionista. He would often say to my sisters and I, "Let's go shopping!" after his appointments. Most often, the exhaustion set in, but he did love a good pair of shoes.

My dad was adamant about being of a clear mind. He did not want the effects of the pain medications that were offered after witnessing my mom go through her days in a non-cognitive state.

Being immune compromised, my dad was susceptible to illness and infection. The doctor said the likelihood of him dying from his disease was unlikely. He would succumb to infection. The diagnosis was correct. He was admitted to Abbotsford Hospital for an infection. After a couple of procedures, it was evident he was not going to be discharged. A family "physician" friend took me aside and explained he was suffering, and pain medication was necessary. However, once he settled with the pain medication, he was going to pass quickly. Oh yes, it did within hours of administering the pain relief. I was inhaling noodles on a mattress in the corner of the room while my sister was speaking with the social workers. At a glance, my sister noticed he stopped breathing, and that was it – he was gone.

My dad was a character. His motto was "attitude is everything"! He is fondly remembered for his sense of humor and caring ways. He was a role model in his community, and his hobby was his highly accomplished career. He would challenge you - taking an easy route was not an option for us. He wanted to leave everyone better than when he met them. He always said everyone must toast me with a good glass of scotch when I go! And that we did!

Full disclosure, I struggled with my dad his last couple of years. He met someone five months after my mom passed, and it was not easy to incorporate a stranger into our world. Deep down, his new love was not the issue. He just had three strong daughters that were not emotionally ready to start a new relationship. It could be seen as selfish, but our family dynamics had been challenged. I wish we had him longer to work through those emotions together. Most importantly, his love was unconditional, and it was felt by all of us.

My world was cracking by the loss of both my mom and dad. I went to the doctor for some help and was prescribed a second anti-depressant to take in the evening. It masked the compounding pain I was trying to escape. The pairing of anti-depressants and wine led me on a journey lapsing in judgment. I was so consumed in escaping from my pain that I was in, that I was estranged from the effects taking its toll on my loved ones.

My husband, Paulo, was obviously worried and made attempts to bring up my drinking from time to time, but obviously, it was not met with an open mind. I was sheepish and embarrassed to discuss it. It made me very defensive. One day I was at work and in my inbox was an email from Paulo. The contents were overwhelming for me as the subject was about my drinking. Obviously, it was not easy for me to have my behavior involving alcohol in print.

When participating in a Zoom call about "my story," Julie said how much he loved me for sending an email creating his dialogue about how he was feeling. Also, how many times did you read it? Very true; I went over it multiple times.

My daughter, Alissa, traveled abroad for years to see the world. She came home for my dad's funeral, and I overheard her say to her siblings, "I had to come home; I didn't want you to go through what I did when Nana died." Inside I thought, what on earth does she mean by that, knowing full well what it meant.

· · ·

March 5, 2017

This date was the day we lost our precious Nonna, my mother-in-law, after a battle with cancer for almost 20 years. Words would not be able to express the strength she showed pre and post cancer. Family was of the utmost most importance to her. She was supportive and showed unconditional love. There was nothing she wouldn't do to keep her family unit together, and she showed it every day in her 74 years of life.

Nonna was the first of my "parents" to start her battle. She underwent surgeries and treatments, always knowing there would be another in a few years. She struggled when my mom was ill and in her final days. She felt guilt that after all her years of battling cancer, her friend was losing her battle sooner. Her compassion for others was genuine and constant.

Obviously, the passing of the matriarch of our family was devasting to all of us. St. Joseph's was overflowing. A tribute to all the lives she touched.

September 30, 2017

This was meant to be a special day. I was with a good friend; we went to the Interior Design show in Vancouver. Driving over the Port Mann Bridge, we noticed a car stopped and slammed on our brakes. Two minutes later, we were involved in an eight-car pileup. We were rear-ended by a truck going 80 km. This collision sent us into a couple of cars and then the meridian. The seats broke on impact, sending us backward.

We were taken by ambulance to Royal Columbian Hospital with concussions and minor injuries. It was a definite set-back. I was home for four months with a concussion that sent me spiraling even further into a depression where wine continued to be my coping mechanism.

My son, Teo, had tried to discuss with me his discomfort with my drinking and how he hurt seeing me this way. He got so frustrated that one day, he blurted out, "You are an alcoholic!"

September 8, 2020

The final of four incredible people in my life to pass. Nonno, my father-in-law, was the eldest of the group, and we treasured his life of 88 years. He was such a character, and we were kindred spirits.

Nonno was devasted at the loss of his beloved wife. Yet, he continued with his journey. He was a master gardener and lived off his harvest for most of the year. He had a reputation for a kick-ass sausage. We treated our portions like treasure.

After becoming ill with what we all thought was a constant flu due to COVID, he was diagnosed with Kidney Cancer. Yes, the "C" word was back. He had his kidney removed and came home to recover. After going through such a traumatic experience, you could see his mind was blurring at times. He went through so much to conquer what the others could not. However, when well enough, he was outside puttering and had a seizure. He was not able to overcome his injuries. I loved that man so much, and his presence is truly missed. He did live his best life.

We had an intimate family service to celebrate his life, and once COVID restrictions lightened up, we had a Celebration for Life on his birthday for family and friends. He was so respected in his community and his family. We had the celebration at our house. I was all business and ready to celebrate this wonderful man until I saw his brother, Uncle Pete, and then I knew this was real, and it happened. I could not hold back the emotions. This release was a start in helping me process.

November 30, 2021

A dear friend of mine told me about a SukJok therapist, Alla Ozerova, whom she knew through friends and had started treatment. SuJok is a healing methodology based on Acupressure that originated in Korea. I pondered it for months and finally made the appointment.

Par for the course, the first session is to find out why you are here and the course of action. The interview was not what I expected. We started talking, and I started to release my emotions, desperately trying to hold back. Knee jerk reaction in our generation to deny our emotions. The therapist explained that the anti-depressants I have been on for over ten years are making me completely numb and unable to process my emotions. Not to mention, my energy level was at an all-time low.

The goal was to move off the anti-depressants! I felt like I was given permission to express my "uncomfortable" emotions. Once accepting this permission, I noticed moments where I was able to weep. After four sessions, it was time for me to take the plunge and eliminate one of the anti-depressants. I was petrified for this to happen. What was I going to be like "Unnumbed"?

I muddled my way through, being very aware of the rawness of my being. Withdrawal hit me hard the first couple of days. Slowly and surely, I have been able to release the layers of sadness that I worked so hard to keep at arms length. It has not been an easy road, but I am going in the right direction. The clarity has shown me I can limit my alcohol intake and not go to the point of no return.

In saying this, in no way am I "anti" anti-depressants. They have a purpose and are prescribed to help people cope in their journey. I still have a journey ahead of me but eliminating one of them allowed me to clear my head and sit with my emotions. This clarity is helping me to realize that releasing this pain is the opening to healing.

May 21, 2022

My daughter, Sophia, now lives in Victoria. We were thick as thieves when she was at home. Because of this distance, at times, I felt disconnected from her, so it was a great opportunity for Sophia and I to spend some bonding time.

I was telling her about the story I am writing and how it has been healing to write my truth. I wanted to start a dialogue with her on how my behavior affected her. During this conversation, she began to tell me about the pressure that was on her dealing with my issue. She worried at night about leaving me. She felt the weight on her shoulders, and it was tough going through those years as a teenager with such worries. Of course, this was a gritty conversation which I needed to hear.

What devastates me is that history is written and cannot be taken back. I am not able to erase those memories for my family, but I can move forward with them, rebuilding the trust that never should have been broken. This is my past, and as much as it affected me, I am not the only one that needs to heal. This story created a platform for my family to show how it affected them.

Present Date

I have been so fortunate to have tremendous support around me. My family and friends watched me go through these difficult times while behaving poorly and being over-indulgent with alcohol. My people who stood by me through those times, even when it was challenging, are still by my side today. I thank all of you for having faith in me and our relationship. My journey to this point would not have been possible without you, and I treasure each and every one of you.

Take Away

The lesson that I learned and want to share is that alcohol and prescription drugs should not be paired as a coping mechanism.

Being present with uncomfortable emotions is the only way to grieve and heal. The process is challenging but dealing with your grief is the only path to moving forward.

Alison DeGianni

...

Sarah Dessen

"There comes a time when the world gets quiet, and the only thing left is your own heart. So, you'd better learn the sound of it. Otherwise, you'll never understand what it's saying."

7

Returning to My Indigenous Culture
HEALED MY HEART

"We may not be responsible for the world that created our minds, but we can take responsibility for the mind with which we create our world." Dr. Gabor Mate

Sometimes, it takes a catalyst to give us a shake, wake us up, to see the bigger picture of what is going on in our lives and how we have been living to bring us to a place of realizing. Wow, I've been doing this thing called life recklessly, without any regard for myself and my future. Something has got to change now!!

This has been my own life experience.

For many years, most of my life, in fact, I was in a place of heaviness, sadness, unhappy. I always felt as though something was missing though if I were asked, I couldn't tell you what I felt was missing. I couldn't name it. I didn't know how to express the emptiness I felt within and how this was what I had always known. I didn't know anything else. I didn't know how to.

I never truly believed full happiness existed as I hadn't ever truly experienced it, and when I did, it was always momentarily.

I would see others, happy, full of life, successful, living life to the fullest, doing all the things they loved and enjoyed, and I'd wonder, how in the heck do they do that, and I can't!

I used to wish for that proverbial magic wand, which of course doesn't exist. Or, that some magical person would come save me from my unhappiness, show me the way to find all the things I had truly believed only existed in the movies, the "happily ever after's."

Coming from an environment with a wealth full of dysfunction. Behaviors, cycles, patterns, abuse of various types, and alcoholism, as well as being a product of and surrounded by residential school survivors. Not understanding back then what colonialism did to my people, the Indigenous culture, connection, spirituality, traditional ways, as well as parenting, now that I understand all of this, it's no surprise I and many others like me experienced and endured all that we did, but we can and do overcome, learn, heal, grow, and succeed. I feel I am proof of that, as are my six children.

As a result of trauma and experiences I had been through, I engaged in the consumption of alcohol from an early age. I recall it was a party going on in my home. When I was five years old that I had my first taste of beer. An adult, thinking it would be funny to see what I thought of the taste, gave me some in a mini colorful "wine glass," the kind that were won back then at carnival games. I remember it well because I thought, ohhhh, I am a big girl now, they let me have beer! I am one of them now. I felt like I now fit in with them because I drank the beer.

I recall little situations like this as a young child with friends. That we would sneak bottles of beer from our parents, who were drinking together, not paying any attention to us at all. We would take the bottles of beer and sit outside underneath the porch steps or nearby within the cover of a bushel of trees or willows and have our own little "drinking party" full of little children who didn't know any better.

We were just modeling what we saw often, and thought was normal behavior. Oh, and there would be cigarettes too, stolen from the drinking adults as well. I don't think we knew how to actually smoke them, but I recall the feeling it gave to be holding that cigarette like an adult would, with our legs crossed, arms folded over, and sucking on that cigarette with the thought we looked all cool and glamourous even, as this is what was often portrayed back then on tv commercials.

My dad left us when I was a toddler. My mom was absent a lot in my early years, so, therefore, I spent a lot of time with my aunts and uncles and sometimes with my grandmother. This was my favorite place to be as my granny took time for me. I felt loved, cared for, and safe. She would sit and tell me stories as she drank her coffee and smoked her extra-long cigarettes. She told me many things as she sipped from her cup of coffee and exhaled large clouds of smoke as I sat and listened intently and also asked a lot of questions.

Many of her stories had to do with our culture and traditions and our spirituality as Indigenous people. I remember she began telling me while I was quite young that I was "gifted." She would tell me I had gifts, that not everyone had these gifts. She said she knew I had gifts as soon as I started talking. I guess I would tell her and my mom things such as knowing things I shouldn't have known and had no way of knowing, as when I shared, they would say no one told her that, so how did she know. I often told them things I would see and hear as well. Often they might be in the same room as me, and I would describe things that to me were happening at that moment, but they couldn't see and hear what I was seeing and hearing.

I often remember my mom would say, don't tell anyone what you know, see, and hear; they will think you are crazy! When I would tell my granny, she would teach me. She would tell me that the things I saw, knew, and heard were not things to be afraid of, that these were my gifts I was born with that Creator had given to me.

She taught me to pray as a toddler. My mom also read me the bible, cover to cover, as, at one point, a bible was the only book we had in the home. My mom's reading to me often and the talks one on one with my granny led to a huge lifelong love of books, as well as an appetite for knowledge.

I recall sitting with my grandmother one day, and she said, "you need to learn to use your gifts, to work with them because you are meant to help people. That is why you are here your purpose". I asked her how I do that and how I am to help people. I remember she told me life would be difficult. You will go through a lot of things that will be hard to live with, but from all of that, you will learn and grow. I will help and teach you along the way. When it is time, you will know.

To me then, her response left a void in my huge curiosity. I wanted to know all the answers, and I wanted to know them now. I wanted to help people even as a child, but I didn't know how and what was meant for me. I remember when I would ask about this, my granny would shrug it off and simply say, "it's not time yet. You have to grow and go through life first. You will know when."

When I was 14, my grandmother, who I also often saw as my protector, my source of love, guidance, attention, support, and a mother figure when my mom was battling her own demons, lost her battle with cancer. When she left our physical world to return to the stars of where we came from, she took all the answers to my questions about "my gifts" and the big secrets to the life that lay ahead in my future, with her. I realized just a few years ago, that I was angry with my granny for passing away and not teaching me and telling me further all the "secrets to my life" that I assumed she held from all her words and stories she told me.

A year before my granny died, I began to actively consume alcohol at the age of 13. I would often run away from home to go party with my friends. I had a group of guy friends I hung around with. I saw all 4 of them as my brothers. They called and treated me like a little sister. I was the only girl in our little group, and I proudly say they treated me like "one of the guys" I fit in perfectly with them. I could be myself. I could talk about and share everything I went through with them. They were there for me with safety, support, and guidance.

They were also my protectors as often I was bullied by other girls in my early teens. I never knew why, often times it happened out of the blue. I was, at times, physically attacked by girls I thought were my friends. To this day, I still don't know how I may have provoked these girls. It seemed they just didn't like me for being, for existing. I always tried my best to get along with them all, to fit in and be accepted. I also was nice when I should not have been and followed along and did what they were doing so that they would accept me and try to ensure I wasn't picked on, bullied, or physically hurt for no reason.

My efforts were futile. I was still bullied and hurt by them. I remember I did ask once why they did these things to me and wanted to hurt me. One of the girls said, "I don't know why but I know that I just don't plain like you, I don't care about you, no one likes or cares about you, and there's nothing you can do about it," as she shoved me and walked away. I remember feeling completely torn, heartbroken even, left wondering what it was about me that they didn't like me, what am I doing or saying wrong, am I dressing funny, am I ugly? They used to tell me this too, that I was ugly, and I believed them.

My group of guy friends, who I saw as my big brothers, they protected me from all these girls in our late teens. Many times, we would be walking along, and it seemed out of nowhere there would be a girl coming at me to yell and swear at me, call me horrible things, attack me in the school field, the streets of downtown, the mall, the arcade, everywhere and anywhere.

I also found adults around this time, in their early to mid '20s, who were young parents, had homes of their own, and liked to party.

They didn't mind having a 13-year-old around to party with them. They accepted her as she was, protected her, and liked to have a young girl around who would clean, wash dishes, cook and take care of their kids as long as they continually gave her a place to sleep when she ran away from home. They would feed her and provide her with alcohol and cigarettes, along with the feelings of acceptance, belonging and care.

Not many knew things I dealt with at home. Where I was supposed to be safe. Where I came from, we were taught from a very early age, often in toddler years... that when we experience or witness wrong doings, abuses, or things that happened behind closed doors when no one is looking or around to see, we keep it to ourselves. If we spoke up, there would be consequences, ones that involved abuse of self or your loved ones.

It was also instilled and conditioned unto us back then that "children were to be seen and not heard," and if a child tried to speak up in an attempt to make a plea for help, it was said they were lying, making things up, attention seeking.... We would be hit then, too, as a form of punishment for "making stories" to be taught a lesson in "crying wolf. I began to experience physical abuse from an uncle as a child.

With him, as I think back, it was never provoked. It would happen out of the blue when he would pick me up and throw me around, against walls and furniture. Kick me while I was on the ground pleading for him to stop, promising I would be good, hit me with an open or closed hand, pull and yank my hair and head around so hard that I felt that not only did my hair and scalp extremely hurt, I felt like my brain was hurting extremely too. I did my best to be on good behavior as I always kept in mind constantly that he could hurt me badly and no one would care or help me. He told me this. He also told me if I told anyone, he would hurt my sister and mom too. I believed him. I kept quiet and didn't say anything for years as I feared my sister and mom being hurt as I was, and everything he did to me hurt badly.

I recall my mom coming home each time and wanting to run to her, to tell her what happened, for her to protect me and make that awful man who was hurting me, though he was my uncle, to go away forever, but I never did because I was scared. I also didn't want him to hurt my mom and my sister. My uncle began to get braver, though there were times my mom and stepdad would be in another room, and he would all of a sudden jump up and start pummeling me.

I learned then that my parents were afraid of him, too, as when I would yell and scream out for help and expect they would kick him out of our home, my stepdad would come running and yell at my uncle, "that's enough now, get off her, leave her alone now!". My uncle would throw one last punch at my head. Then he would walk off and sit at the kitchen table where my parents were and have coffee with them like nothing had happened.

He had once held a knife to my throat when I was 15. I locked myself in a bedroom and called my cousin on the phone, who came running to my house to save and protect me. She was younger than me but not afraid of anyone or anything, she had her family who could and would protect her in every way they may need to, and this was well known in our family.

Another time I recall vividly I was sitting at the kitchen table doing homework, my little sister, who was seven at the time, and I was 14, was sitting at the table as well. Our uncle was behind me at the kitchen sink washing dishes, all was well, or so it had seemed until… something hit me hard on the back of the head. I never saw it coming. I came to on the dining room floor with a very sore head and wondering what had happened as my sister sat at the table crying hysterically. When I looked up, my uncle stood over me with a cast iron frying pan in his hand. He had hit me in the back of the head with it.

My sister had made mention of this a couple of times throughout the years. She said she was traumatized by having seen this happen as she recalled that she thought I was dead. She thought our uncle had killed me as I didn't move or come to for a long time. This, too, we never spoke of or told anyone.

When I was 16, after yet another attack by my uncle, I decided to fight back. I yelled at him, I told him he couldn't do this to me anymore, I told him I was calling the police to report him, and I did. He left my home out of fear of the police, they came, but nothing happened. He did leave me alone after this incident, finally.

When I was 18, I had my first son, and I feared my uncle even knowing that my child was mine. I didn't want him to go after my son just because he was mine. I didn't want my child to ever be hurt in any way by another. I remember when my son was two, my uncle returned to the community to visit family. I felt instant fear knowing he was around, but now I was a mom with a child to protect. I told my family that if the uncle asked who the little boy was, not to say he was mine as I feared he might hurt him. Long before this, I had the mindset that it was me against the world. If I didn't find ways to protect and stand up for myself, no one else was going to protect me, take care of me, or save me from being hurt.

Not only was it my uncle who was physically abusive, often times I had babysitters who could be just as bad. At seven years old, I had a babysitter slap me across the face because I didn't want to share my ice cream cone with her. Back then, my mom could be just as awful with her only known form of punishment too, which included anything that was near, such as broom handles, belts, sticks, spatulas, shoes, hangers, anything, as well as her hands. I had my share of items broken over my back and my bottom by then, even at seven years old.

On this day with the babysitter, when she slapped me, I laughed at her instead of crying. She hit me harder and repeatedly, attempting to get a reaction out of me and make me cry. I continued to laugh harder and repeatedly told her to hit me again. By this time, I was so tired of being hit all the time I started to think that maybe if I didn't cry each time and laughed instead, acted like I wasn't being hurt, maybe it would stop.... It didn't.

As I began to have relationships, I found I attracted abusive men. By this time, it was well ingrained within me that I was to do as I was told, listen and not speak or express myself, that I was alone in the world, that I was never safe and had no one to help and protect me. That I was truly alone in the world. And I believed this fully.

As I had more children throughout the years, I became hyper-vigilant about protecting my own children. I realize now I was ultra-protective of my younger sister and my baby brother too. I never wanted them to experience the hurt and pain I lived with on a daily basis. I did my best to protect them all. I always feared they would be hurt by someone and not be able to tell me, so I went out of my way to keep them close where I could protect them and to ensure they were never alone with anyone I felt I couldn't trust. Today, I am still like this with my own children.

My two youngest struggle with speech, being special needs. I don't leave them with anyone unless it's my closest trusted family as I carry this fear still strongly that someone could hurt my child and they wouldn't be able to tell me. I know if this happened, it would tear me apart as I think back on all the hurt I myself experienced and how often throughout life, I would wish the earth would just open up and swallow me whole, so I wouldn't have to live with hurt and pain anymore.

Despite all of this, in my mid-teens, I loved school. Oh, the stories I could tell, both good and bad, of all I experienced in school from the days as a young child. I was hungry at times as there was little to no food at home often that I would take my time to put on my outdoor shoes when the recess bell rang so that I would be the last one in the classroom as all the kids rushed outside to play. So that I could quickly look in their backpacks and lunch boxes to steal little bits of food from each, hoping not to be caught, and quickly eating what little treasures I could find. I remember my stomach being so empty and hurting at times because it needed food. I recall the sheer happiness of having been able to feed myself and soothe the sometimes extreme hunger pain I would have.

I did get caught finally, though. I had to go to the office with the principal, where at first, I was getting into trouble. They asked me why I was stealing from the kid's backpacks and lunchboxes. I put my head down in shame and embarrassment as I had tears rolling down my cheeks. I answered that I was hungry and that it hurt, and I didn't know how to get food.

After the day I was caught stealing food, the principal would come to get me each morning. I would be taken to the infirmary, where I was well fed a good breakfast. The first time they came to get me from class, I was afraid. When I got to the infirmary and saw the food and that it was for me, I was so happy and ate everything quickly. I was then told too that when the bell would ring at lunch time, I was to come back here. There would be food waiting for me for lunch each day too. I was so happy. I felt on top of the world. I didn't have to be hungry and steal anymore, someone cared about me. When the kids would ask where I was going, I would tell them I didn't feel good.

Today, I am a thin woman. I have been this way for many years. I have had rude comments made to me as to why I am thin. I sometimes forget to eat. My children now ask me at times if I have eaten, especially when they know I have had a busy day. Over the years, I have learned that my body has become accustomed for so long that if I don't eat when I first feel hunger, the feeling passes, and I will forget that I haven't eaten. When I realize now that I haven't fed myself, I am quite conscious of this past and how it affects me still, so I will ensure I eat right away when the thought crosses my mind. It's not something I can help. I have tried. It is how my body developed itself to cope with the environments I was in. I have found that when I quit drinking, it became much harder to gain and keep any weight on. I realize that what weight I did gain as an alcoholic may have been, in fact, bloat.

School was my happy place, too, a safe space. I was accepted and a part there. I belonged. In junior high, I was in classrooms for young teens like me a few times a day, the "gifted classes," I was on the honor roll, I was on the student leadership and debate teams, and I skipped two grades as the work was too easy for me and I was breezing through it all quickly.

The principal would talk with me at times. He would tell me how bright and intelligent I was. He would tell me I could do and be anything I wanted to be in life, with the brains and smarts I had. I didn't know back then what an IQ was, but he said I had a high one. I told him I wanted to be a doctor. I was also able to share with him the life I was dealing with outside of school, all the obstacles, adversities, challenges, and abuses. He would check on me from time to time, and he also began sending me to the school guidance counselor on a regular basis.

The principal took seriously my dream to be a doctor. He would take me aside at times to talk. He was developing and laying out an academic plan for me to be able to pursue my dreams. He would tell me how this was possible, what I needed to do, and how I would likely get into any college or university I might choose. I was excited at the prospects and possibilities of all of this. I began to dream often about what my future and life as a doctor might be like.

This was short-lived, though, as my parents decided it was time for our family to move back to our home community. A very small isolated Indigenous community which at the time, had nothing to offer me education wise, or at least, that was my belief. I was heartbroken. The school suggested that my parents find somewhere I could live without having to move with them so that I could continue my education with them and, continue to be groomed and guided towards my goal and dream of becoming a doctor. My mom chose against this, and away we moved. School was different than what I was used to in an urban community where I had lived for so many years.

There were many aspects that were missing, and I was extremely unhappy again. I felt I didn't belong or fit in, and within a few months of beginning school, I dropped out until I was 18 and was able to attend the community "college" and enrolled in Adult Basic Education to begin and finish where I left off in high school. With my moving, my goal and dream of becoming a doctor went out the window, as did my care about my future.

Often, I was told in my younger years when I was doing well, that people like me (Indigenous) weren't supposed to succeed. When I did something well, I was asked who I thought I was. Did I think that I was good now or better than everyone else? These comments hurt, so I began to hide my accomplishments and smarts. I had come to believe that my intelligence and smarts were not good things, they were not acceptable, that they would be cause in some way, shape, or form of hurt and pain from others toward me.

As I think back, in my adult years chasing a career and deciding what I wanted to be when I "grew up," I saw an ad in the newspaper. An advertisement for an information session for possible future corrections officers. I went to the information session, and I learned about the role and responsibilities of an officer within this field, and the education involved to get there.

The training was happening in my community, was financially covered for anyone who was chosen to attend, and on top of this, you would be paid to attend training. I applied, and I was a successful candidate. I trained, I wanted this and badly. It meant the possibility of a long-time stable career, financial stability, benefits, and the possibility of helping others in this capacity.

I always kept my granny's words "that I was to help people, this was my purpose here, and that one day I would know when it was time."

I thought maybe this was how I was meant to help people, and I had to find out. I worked hard on all assignments and physical training. I graduated. My children and their father were the only people who attended my graduation. As proud of me as they were, and I was of myself, I felt I had done something hugely horribly wrong by succeeding. Wild to think back at how hugely I was conditioned to this belief that for me, success was not success. It was a failure and disappointment, to my extended family.

Going back to alcohol... I had learned to escape with booze. If I was hurting, there was beer. If something bad happened or someone passed away, there was booze to soothe me. Heck, even when good things happened and were to be celebrated, it was time for booze. If I wanted to relax, to forget things, to feel a sense of normalcy, to speak up when I was afraid to or to confront someone who hurt me, there was alcohol to give me that boost and courage.

Alcohol didn't hurt or use me, cause me pain, at least in the moments that I was actively engaging with it. It didn't judge me. It didn't say mean things and call me names. It didn't accuse me of untruthful things. It just sat there silently, accepting me openly, allowing me to indulge in what I saw then as its satisfying comforts, soothing me, helping me to escape life momentarily and to forget everything I faced and dealt with, to forget my past for a little while.

By this time, I was very well entrenched in a mindset and experience that there was no such thing as happiness. If happiness was experienced, it was short-lived, and often, something bad always followed, so I would be in a place of expectation, prepared, and ready for the bad that was to come. I also believed that success wasn't meant for me. I would never find or have it. I was not meant to.... Why I didn't know. I just knew it wasn't supposed to happen for me.

Many things not mentioned here happened throughout the years, both good and bad. I had noticed that the good things were starting to outweigh the bad and heaviness. I was starting to experience happiness more often, I was starting to taste what success was with my newfound career, and I enjoyed it. I was happy that the father of my children and I were able to give our children many things that I never had growing up. I also, and to this day, overcompensated when I shopped for groceries. I never wanted my children to open a fridge or cupboard door to find them empty. I never wanted them to know the pain and despair feelings of hunger.

Though life was beginning to shift slowly, things were looking better and better all the time, and life was improving. My children were happy, or so I thought. I would still, in a moment of hardship, hurt, difficulty, and even happiness, too, engage in alcohol. I would leave my children home so that I could go out drinking. Sometimes for a day, or two, or three. I never stopped to consider how my kids were affected. I did think of them and wonder what they were up to while I was gone, but I didn't come home then as my relationship with their father was in a very bad place, falling apart quickly.

Their father, too, was an alcoholic. Drinking brought many problems to my relationship over the years. And believe it or not, I never ever did cheat on my spouse. Cheating was something I never believed in. I was also raised that this was hugely wrong and a huge sin by my granny while she was alive. I did at times, come out of a blackout or a pass out to being abused in horrible ways. I was put into situations where I was overpowered and allowed people to hurt me because I couldn't get out of the situations and just wanted them to quickly get it over with so I could get away. Abuses of various types continued in my home and elsewhere when alcohol was involved.

My relationship fell apart completely. I then got involved with a couple of other men who were hugely abusive physically, mentally, emotionally, and even at times, spiritually, too, as the things I sometimes experienced actually felt to have broken my spirit. I thought I would never recover fully or be able to overcome. I began to experience three-day hangovers, and still, I did it anyway though I knew I was going to be extremely ill, unable to function as all I wanted to do was sleep. I began to grow tired of this life but still, I couldn't stop. When my oldest son was 18, I began to drink with him and thought no wrong of it at all. Sometimes his friends would join us. This was short-lived, thankfully, as, the following year, I quit completely.

I recall waking up in the middle of the night once, after having been drinking earlier in the day, after a vivid dream. In this dream, there was an old wrinkled Indigenous woman, dressed in clothing from another era, with a braid in her hair, talking to me. She was pointing her finger at me as she loudly and sternly said, "If you don't smarten up and quit this drinking of yours, you will be dead soon. What will happen to your kids" and that's all I remember of the dream. It shook me to the core, and it scared me. It made me think deeply of my children and how they were being affected, what was to become of them, their future, and my future.

I slowed down a little, but I didn't stop. I couldn't stop. I began reaching out to counselors, even to doctors, for help. Once when I was sharing with a doctor, I told him I had heard of a pill that was given to alcoholics who couldn't stop drinking that helped them to stop. I asked for this. He said he would look into this, and he did. He called me soon after to tell me that such a thing did exist. However, it was only available in Australia.

I asked my counselor to help me get into a treatment program two years before I finally attended one. There was a long waiting list with a minimum of six months which seemed like an eternity. Though I was beginning to feel desperation for help, that my life was spiraling out of control, I continued to turn to drinking. I continued to have difficult, hurtful experiences.

Within this time, unbeknownst to me, I was given the date rape drug on a few occasions by different people. Once, I knew something was wrong as the way I was feeling and what I was experiencing didn't add up to the feeling I knew I should have had after just two beers. I got myself out of the party as I was lapsing into a feeling of the worst being horribly different and something hugely wrong in the moment. I got myself to what I thought was a safe place, as the man who gave it to me in a drink followed me closely behind. When I got to this particular place, I wasn't completely coherent as the drug was taking its full effects, and I was trying to explain what was happening to me, and I guess I was slurring my words.

The police were called, and I was taken to a jail cell that night which I was okay with cause at least I was safe. I later found out that when I went to this place in need of and trying to find help, I was video recorded in this state, and it was shown to many people I work with.

I was called in by my bosses for a meeting where I was told I may also be facing reprimand for my "questionable behavior" as a public servant. I had to go in and shamefully explain what had taken place. I had been in a very bad car accident with friends, to this day it amazes me that we all walked away with minor injuries. I seemed too often be in the wrong places with super bad timing too. I witnessed many things take place, people doing wrongful things, and somehow, they would often include me when they told their stories, so this led to me being accused of things many times that I knew well I had nothing to do with.

I also got into trouble with the law for the first time, gaining myself a DUI charge and license suspension. I was so lost. I felt I had no hope at all. I wished for miracles, and I never did let my grand-mother rest. For all the years she has been passed on, I always spoke to her, asking her to help me, to lead, and to show me what I needed to do to get out of and change this life I had been leading.

Amidst all this chaos, I had a baby boy, my 5th son. I had no trouble quitting drinking when learning of pregnancies throughout the years. I had a healthy pregnancy, and all was well. Then when my newborn son was 15 minutes old, I was told it was suspected he had down syndrome. When he was three months old, this was confirmed.

My son was tiny, he had difficulty feeding, and so he had to be syringe fed the first few months of life. He and his well-being were my full focus, my world. I swore my life was going to change now for the rest of my life as this little boy needed me, and he needed me fully healthy. I focused on him fully. I did all that I could to give him a better life then I was told he would lead shortly after he was born, to ensure he thrived in all ways. And he did, hugely. I was so proud of my baby son and all he was accomplishing that I was told he might never. This, too, though, didn't stop me for too long.

When my son was a year and a half old, I began drinking regularly again, and with that, my life and my world began to spiral out of control. I then noticed, too, that my oldest son was struggling and experiencing so many obstacles and troubles, hurt and pain due to the alcoholism that was beginning to take over his life. It hurt me so much to see all he was going through and dealing with. The realization that I, and his father, taught him these ways of living, he saw it as normal as he didn't really see another way ever modeled for him without alcohol involved.

I realized that I, unaware unconsciously, had passed on the "invisible emotional baton" to my son. To all my children, filled with all the generational trauma, behaviors, patterns, and cycles that had years ago and unbeknownst back then to my mother had been passed down to me. Seeing all of this going on around me, looking at my other younger children and stopping in a moment with the fearful thought of, oh my god, what am I creating and teaching my kids here? Holy shit, they are slowly but surely becoming who I never wanted to be, but I am, and I am teaching them this, that it is normal and okay, that this is what life is supposed to be, when I know full well that it's not.

This is when I truly started pushing to be sent off to an alcohol treatment center. Now I was completely desperate to change my life for my children. I didn't want them to be who I had become. I was ashamed of who I was. I didn't want to live this way anymore. I wanted my boys to be mentally, emotionally, physically, and spiritually healthy young men. To one day be the amazing husbands and fathers I never had but would see in the movies and read about in books, but the way I was going, I didn't see this happening. I foresaw their futures as the complete opposite if I didn't do something to change it quickly.

I reached out again to a counselor, this time with extreme desperation. I needed to get into a treatment center as soon as possible. It took 2/3 weeks, but now, things were moving along quickly, and I knew it was just a short time till I was there. I had asked if I could attend a center in Edmonton as this was the place my granny had attended and gained her own sobriety and then her certification as an addiction's counselor. My mother had also attended and gained her sobriety in the same place. I wanted to go to and follow in the footsteps of both the women I saw as my superheroes, after all they had been through, endured and overcome.

I also chose this place as it was the only one, I found then that integrated Indigenous culture and spirituality into its healing programs. When I first got there, I was adamant I wasn't there to quit drinking. I was there to work on my past, everything I had carried throughout life that was having huge effects on not only me but my children now too.

During the third week there, my thoughts changed completely. I had done so much work and learned so much about why I and my life were the way they were. I wanted so badly to understand and overcome that I worked so hard to learn all I could. I also asked for homework and reading material so that I could immerse myself during off programming hours.

I also credit my change of mind and heart about gaining sobriety to the counselor I lucked out with. She was from a difficult past, too, full of many similar life experiences as me. Many of the people that were there to find and gain recovery. Her self-disclosure, compassion, and understanding on every possible level of why we were the way we were and lived all the years as we had. She had been in those exact places too and overcame them all, lived to tell about it, and now shares and helps others, too, which is what got through to me hugely and fully. She had true lived experience. If not for her, I sometimes wonder if I would have found and maintained sobriety since attending.

Often people that know me say I healed myself. I have to admit that beyond the doors of that treatment center, living in a community where the resources and supports were minimal, I overall did. It took returning to my Indigenous culture, ceremony, traditions, ways, spirituality, self-disciple, tons of will power, and moments of weakness that I often fought through the first year or two. Books by Eckhart Tolle, Deepak Chopra, Dr. Gabor Mate, Wayne Dyer, Don Miguel Ruiz, Colin Tipping, among many others. Podcasts, everything and anything I could get my hands on involving wellbeing, self-help, and healing. But most of all, my immense love for my children and wanting them to live the best lives they can.

I also learned all I could about universal/natural law and how this all is a world of connection and cause and effect. I had to learn about and fully understand trauma on all levels as well, how and why it affects us and stays with us long term, and how it affects our lives in every way. How it affected mine. I grew such a passion for trauma and healing work that one of the things I chased was training in trauma, addictions, healing, and Compassionate Inquiry taught by and based on the teachings of Dr. Gabor Mate, which I had completed and graduated from.

I have also learned that I live with complex post-traumatic stress disorder due to a series of repeated lifelong traumatic events, being in autopilot and survival mode for most of my life before I found sobriety. I have learned the differences between PTSD and CPTSD, how to work with this in my life, what I need to do for my own self-care, and even as a helper of others. I sometimes need to reach out for support for myself too.

I was out driving one day with my younger brother on the highway. We were mostly sitting in silence as we listened to music we both enjoyed. Little did he know I was lost in thought, maybe even in another "world," for lack of a word, as we drove along. I suddenly broke the silence and started to share with my brother a vision I had while we were out there on the highway and sat in silence.

I had seen the experiences of my mother, her mother, and women before them that also lived difficult lives. I was told and shown why this took place, why it was continuing within my own family, and how and why I needed to break all of these cycles and patterns, how it was so important, and what could be for my own children if I didn't make the change. With tons of tears as I shared with my brother what I was just shown in vision, I told him, "I get it now, I understand!" "I know what needs to be done and how to break this finally!" "Now that this was given to me, I have to follow through. If I don't, someone else might not!!!". I haven't, and won't forget, what I was shown out there. I share sometimes with others of my vision if I feel they will get something out of it or that it will help them in some way.

Two years into my sobriety, I laid down early one evening for a nap. I had a vivid dream of my granny and her sisters who are with her in the spirit world. I woke up so excited about this dream, it was so vivid, and I remembered it so clearly, I had to share with someone. I didn't see it as a dream but as a visit that took place while I was in dreamtime, from my loved ones in the spirit world. I was so excited and moved by this dream that, I had tears of happiness streaming down my face as I told the father of my children all about it.

It's been five years now since this dream, but what I do remember is my great aunt, who was alive when my Dakota was born. She had never got to meet him before she passed but would often call to ask how he was doing. When I saw my aunt in this dream, she had an excited expression on her face as she exclaimed happily, "I saw him" she said this a couple of times, and I asked "who." She told me she had finally got to see and meet my Dakota. She and my granny said that they visited with him often, that they lead and teach him things. What he needs to know to get through this physical life as one born with special needs. I fully know this to be truth as Dakota has displayed and shown us within my family, what he knows, that he has never seen or been told of before.

My older children used to mention some of the things Dakota does as odd and ask me why he does the things he sometimes does. I've shared and taught my older boys about this, shared my dream with them, and have taught them not to question or point out certain things as being different, as there is a reason Dakota does these things. He should be encouraged to develop these instead of being taught to see them as out of the ordinary. My granny told me a lot about Dakota. She told me she sent him to me because I needed him and that he needed me. She told me she chose well as I have been doing great with him. She told me Dakota doesn't speak because he knows things that I, as well as the world, are not yet ready for. She told me of things that were to come for myself, for my children too. She told me she was proud of me, that she has been and will continue to be with me every step of the way to help, lead, guide, and support me.

When Dakota was six years old, I learned I was carrying another child. I learned at ten weeks along that this child I carried was yet another boy, son number six. I also learned then, at ten weeks along, that he would have down syndrome, too, though I have been told and am often reminded by people of how rare this is for a mother to birth two children who both carry the genetic makeup, the extra chromosome, that results in down syndrome.

With my youngest, I was instantly thrown into a world of chaos, learning, growth, and healing shortly after finding that I was carrying him. I see my youngest as, though I carried and birthed him, am raising him, he chose me as his mother... he didn't choose a life in this physical world to be here for me, I believe he came for his brother Dakota and why he is special needs too. They will always have one another for life. They will grow, learn, thrive, and accomplish together and always have a companion in one another. They both have taught and grown me, as well as their brothers, and our family, in huge ways. I look forward to the future that lay ahead of us all and what is yet to be learned and accomplished.

I see my experiences, both good and heavy ones too, as gifts now. I can see the bigger, deeper picture that most wouldn't see or understand of why I went through all that I did, with a purpose. To be a helper in this life, I need to be able to relate to and fully understand others and their personal experiences from and on all levels, with full compassion and non-judgment. I believe without my life experiences and my personal journey through a life of difficulty, pain, and unhappiness, I would not have all the qualities I have now to be able to help others.

Nowadays, I am constantly involved in projects of various types. I sit on a board of directors of an organization that help women across the country from different walks of life who are living in and dealing with similar circumstances as I had in my past. I sometimes share my personal story within groups to help people to see that they are not alone. There are many of us out there who have been to and through hell, found our ways out of its flames, and have overcome fully to succeed. To show them that if I was able to do this, to be where I am today and do all that I do, that they can too. I give talks on trauma education and healing when asked. I also engage in a hobby of Indigenous beadwork when I have the time, I have recently gotten involved with modelling and sharing a stage with amazing women I have followed for years on social media, I have been an extra for a tv pilot, along with the daily single-handed care and responsibilities of my two little boys who live with special needs.

I don't know what will be, what else is to come in this life, but I do know my healing journey is lifelong. We are always experiencing, learning, growing, and healing. It's what life is about. It never ends. Will I ever let my granny rest peacefully... I haven't for the past 30 years since she has passed, and I don't intend to stop asking her for her help and guidance in this life when I need it, and I believe she will walk along my side until it is my time to join her back among the stars. I sometimes wish I could see ahead to what is to come, but where would the fun, the lessons, teachings, growth, and blessings in that be. After all, it's why we are here in this life, to learn and grow. If I don't do much else in this life, I will be okay with that. I know I have accomplished and overcome a lot... so far.

I have helped numerous amounts of people in various ways and will continue to when the opportunity arises. If anything, I broke generations of trauma, abuse, alcoholism, and addictions for my own children and for my future grandchildren. That in itself is a huge purpose as in my being chosen by each of my children as their mother, and I accomplished this. For me, that is legacy enough to leave for my children. I also have done something I used to believe I never could or would. I've made my mother proud more times than I can count. I have received that "unseen" diploma in the best school I think there is, the school of life experiences and triumph through obstacles and adversities.

Colinda Laviolette

...

Colleen Hoover

"Life is a funny thing. We only get so many years to live it, so we have to do everything we can to make sure those years are as full as they can be. We shouldn't waste time on things that might happen someday, or maybe even never."

8

Cultivate Resilience
HEAL FROM THE WOUND, GROW FROM THE SCAR

"I can be changed by what happens to me. But I refuse to be reduced by it." - Maya Angelou

I f I had been someone more in tune with their body, I may have learned much earlier that having pain in my stomach prior to challenging events, like writing university exams, or to joyful events, like my 21st birthday or family reunions, was not exactly normal. Nor was the urge to always need the washroom prior to heading out the door, or the uncontrollable retching that could occur suddenly a few hours after eating. In hindsight, it was not normal.

Yet like most people in their twenties, I believed I knew how life worked. I graduated high school, having kept my permanent record squeaky clean, decided what I wanted to do with the rest of my life, obtained a university degree, found a career, fell in love, married, and then planned to have a family.

Well, that's when my life went cattywampus. I married with the belief that it was forever. It was if forever qualifies as seven years. I had always, to that point, believed that if we loved each other, no matter what, we could make it work. That was youthful naivety.

I had not realized yet, that both people had to want the same thing and be moving and growing in the same general direction. After you have that, then love is the choice that holds it together. Our relationship came to an impasse when we started active attempts to have children. This ultimately required us to dip our toes into fertility treatments.

One month into treatments and pow, my husband withdrew from participating. We argued and then we were silent.

Frequently, my career took me out of town. Getting back after a work trip, my husband had planned a dinner out for us to celebrate my 31st birthday. It was a lovely restaurant, full of leafy green trees and twinkling lights that provided dining privacy. The menu promised delicious courses paced well to allow for in-depth conversation.

Knowing that our relationship was strained, I was silently enjoying the uncommon thoughtfulness of my husband's choice to celebrate my birthday. That feeling lasted through the salad course and splashed into the soup. He wanted a divorce.

Through tears and reminiscence of our good times and those that were not so good, we acknowledged that love still existed between us. I was willing to keep working on our relationship, but only if both of us were doing the work.

My husband stated he was not so willing and chose to move out the next day to live at his mother's home. That accommodation lasted only an obligatory few weeks until he moved in with his girlfriend.

By then, however, I was past being hurt. He had made a choice. I was probably numb and pragmatic. My concern now was finding the best opportunity to disappoint my parents. At the time, my parents had been married for 33 years, and I was going to tell them that I could not even make seven years work. Surprisingly, I was prepping for a disappointment that was all in my head. Interesting how so many stories that we tell ourselves, give us distress and worry, and yet usually do not reflect reality or turn out the way we think.

My parents were certainly concerned about me and my emotional state, but only wanted the best for me and were supportive of my new single status. Divorce, of course, involves not only splitting the relationship and making announcements to all concerned but also splitting the assets. This meant we had to arrange to sell our home, find alternate places to live and move.

Shortly after my birthday and our divorce decision, the pain in my lower abdomen became worst and was no longer intermittent, but constant. Packing and moving became much more challenging. My husband tried to help separate our things and pack, but the one afternoon he was to put things in boxes, he spent in mopey, teary-eyed reminiscence. I sent him away. This task needed clear and determined logic to be completed and my ex-husband's sentimentality was only prolonging the job.

During this disruptive time of selling my home and moving, I had visited doctors and specialists and done all the less invasive upper and lower GI tests. None provided any certainty of a diagnosis. The suggested possibilities ranged from cysts to ulcers

Finally, I had an interview with a surgeon who showed me an x-ray of stones in my gallbladder. He said that this was the cause of my pain. However, since gallstone surgery was not considered an emergency, he would need to check for a time when he could schedule the OR. It would probably be in a few months. He then asked me to sign the authority to have my gallbladder removed.

Not an emergency! I had been in pain, living on Tylenol 3's, like they were candy since May. The thought of waiting a few more months was frustrating and energy draining. I did not want to imagine how much pain I could be trying to manage by then.

I was not completely convinced it was my gallbladder either. I verified with the surgeon, the location of the culprit organ. He pointed to the upper right side of my torso. "So then, why, if it is my gallbladder," I asked, "is my pain below my belly button on my left side?" The surgeon shrugged and shook his head saying that there was nothing else indicated on the test results.

Taking a slow, deep breath, I acknowledged that now was better than later to remove gallstones because the prognosis does not improve as one gets older. I understood that a person can have a relatively normal life without a gallbladder. However, I wanted the surgeon to know that I instinctively knew it was not my gallbladder causing the pain. Although, I signed the authorization for surgery, I requested he assure me that while in my abdomen, he would also look lower for alternative causes of my pain.

I spent the next 2 months with increasing pain, getting through the workday, foggy on pain medication and still no call from the doctor regarding a surgery date. By mid July, I could not stand the pain any longer. I made two decisions. First, I was going to check into the hospital as an emergency case, and second, I made sure to sign my divorce papers before being admitted to the hospital in case something was to happen.

I was afraid. Probably more afraid than I had ever been in my life. Other than visiting relatives, I had never spent any time in a hospital in my 31 years, not even in the emergency room. And the idea of death was uncomfortable and unfamiliar because it was not a topic we discussed around our family dinner table, where nothing was a taboo subject. My limited experience with dealing with death was my attendance at a couple of funerals, a school acquaintance and a friend's mom. Both sad situations of them passing sooner that they should have.

Likely, I entertained this strong fear of dying because I had not received a definitive diagnosis. Therefore, the result of this surgery was open to all possibilities that my imagination chose to dream up. I worried about the surgery, about surviving the surgery, or worst, about getting a terminal diagnosis after the surgery. I had to find something to calm my mind.

Being a reader, the self-help section of my favorite New Age bookstore introduced me to Louise Hay and her book, You Can Heal Your Body. I started learning to visualize, to use affirmations, and to believe that I had control over my feelings. I could choose how to feel in a specific present moment. In turn, my feelings could set up a calm healing environment in my body.

This is where I went, into my head, as I was prepped for surgery. "I am safe," I said to myself. As the gurney rolled down the corridor with the view of each passing fluorescent light, "I will heal." As warm blankets were laid on me in pre-op, "I am secure in the surgeon's hands." I was so much in my head that one of the OR nurses checked on me because I was so quiet and calm on the monitors. I told her I was doing my mantras. She smiled and nodded.

I awoke in my hospital bed because a phone was ringing. My brother was calling to see how the operation went. I could hear my friend, who was waiting at my bedside, answer the call and say that I had not yet heard the diagnosis. This perked me up, and I told my friend to go ahead and tell my brother whatever the doctor had said.

Guess what, it wasn't the worst news that I had been dreading. It turned out to be Crohn's disease and the surgeon was confident that he had found and removed all of it. Even in my groggy post-op state, I no longer felt that constant pain of the past months. Sure, there was incision pain, but it was different. The nagging pain in my gut was gone and that was enough for me. I silently thanked the universe for getting me this far. I was young and knew I could heal.

I just had to spend a couple of weeks being the most interesting surgical case on the ward during my recovery. I had oxygen tubes and throat tubes to prevent stomach reflux, drain tubes in my side, and staples along an S-like incision. I chose not to look for myself, as the faces of those who visited struggled to smile and look hopeful yet reflected that all they saw was me in the middle of a freaking mess of medical equipment and surgical dressings.

Just a friendly hint, if you want to keep any semblance of modesty, do not be an interesting surgical patient.

For most of my stay, there was a steady parade of surgical residents through my hospital room, viewing my incision, looking at the drains and charts, and asking about how I was feeling. A Crohn's diagnosis was a rarity, apparently, in 1989. My gown was more up than down, such a medical curiosity. I quickly learned to disconnect from the daily inspections and focused only on the residents' conversations.

Walking soon after surgery was not as much of a thing as it is today, but I was walking within a week. I used a visualization that saw my body heal from the inside out in my mind. I surprised even the doctors with my speedy recovery and was released from the hospital almost a week earlier than they had expected.

Life slowly returned to normal, to being single, and being focused towards building my career as a corporate trainer. Yet life would upheave again when my local corporate office closed, and I chose to follow and move with the company to another city. It was an easy decision to make. My family was the only link to stay and work in with an airline made living in another place a non-issue. I could fly home in a couple of hours whenever it was necessary. I was ecstatic to live in a city where the sea meets the mountains and the sky. I was soon promoted, and my career continued on track.

A couple of years later, I found love again, married and within that year we were blessed with a daughter, our most precious of life's gifts. She had a dramatic entrance into the world. All things went smooth with the pregnancy until her due date. She probably liked her womb accommodations so much that she was not ready to be born yet. I was tasked to come to the hospital every couple of days to monitor my blood pressure levels and her heart rate. By the time she was two weeks overdue, my doctor said that it was time. My blood pressure was getting dangerously high, and I should be admitted to the hospital to be induced the next day.

My birthing experience was unusual, more frantic excitement than serenity. The induction medication did not seem to work and after 18 hours I had not dilated more than a couple of centimeters. The baby was being stubborn. Unbeknownst to me, the doctors were concerned for both me and the baby due to my ever increasing blood pressure. The doctors had told my father and husband that they could not tell me this was happening because the doctors did not want me upset since this might further boost my blood pressure levels. However, I could see something was not right.

Monitors were being attached to the baby's head, my water was broken, and epidural procedures began. I asked my husband what was wrong, but he could only say it was going to plan, the preparation for a possible C-section.

With such a gaggle of medical staff in my room, one nurse tripped over the monitor lead on my baby's head and set off all kinds of bells and whistles on the machines. This brought more anxious looking doctors to the room. I signaled to my husband to remove my oxygen mask so I could tell him not to fuss, everything was ok. That it was only a pulled lead and to have them check that the head monitor was still attached.

With the epidural in, it was an easy decision to infuse the correct anesthetic to facilitate a C-section. Within 40 mins our beautiful daughter was born. I could not see the procedure due to a surgical screen, but I could feel pulling and tugging in my abdomen while my husband, who was standing by my head, held my hand. When we both heard her cry, we knew she was perfect. Once cleaned and swaddled, I saw her big bright eyes peeking from under the blanket. I was hooked and bonded in an instant.

Unfortunately, I could not hold her for another day as they treated my blood pressure. That night I had what I thought was a dream but may have been drug induced, where the fields were beautiful green and the sky a brilliant blue. But there was no sound. Complete silence. I was so peaceful and content here in this field and wanted to stay. After strolling through the grass and wildflowers forever, a single thought seemed to snatch me away from the field. "I cannot stay, my daughter needs me."

After a week in the hospital, our little family came home, with all efforts focused on learning how to keep our new human happy, healthy, and safe. We settled into family, work, and raising our daughter. Our life ebbed and flowed with struggle and joy mingled together as it should.

After our daughter had grown and found her own life partner, my husband and I started to ponder what retirement might be like. But believe it or not, I had more to learn about healing and resilience.

Shortly after celebrating 36 years with my company, I again felt completely unwell. There was a frequent heaviness in my abdomen, and I was often fatigued no matter how much rest I took. It was not intense pain like the first time, but a deep sagging lethargy. Medical tests and multiple ultrasounds were inconclusive.

Over the years, I had little concern about my previous Crohn's experience returning. I had had a baby, and regular medical check-ups, and nothing seemed a miss. Yet this lack of diagnosis seemed to be a pattern. Crohn's can be sneaky in all its forms.

Attempting to refresh and rejuvenate, I had taken a two-week vacation to glamp in our RV in the woods. Unfortunately, I spent the entire vacation like a zombie, sleeping almost all the time. My instinct said to take this seriously, so once again I decided to admit myself into the emergency room. A whole day of tests and CT scans showed multiple fissures and bacterial abscesses. I was scheduled for surgery the very next day.

This time I was not afraid. Of course, I did not look forward to the unknown new procedures or possible results of a second surgery, but I knew that I needed to get better. It would be ok. It had been 29 years since my last episode, so treatments for Crohn's must have improved. Also, my surgeon was quite youthful, and more likely to know the newest advanced treatments and surgical techniques for my condition.

The experience of my first surgery gave me a comfort level and knowledge to ask questions about my treatment and recovery for this second time under the scalpel. This time I had more drains and a few days after the surgery endured a second procedure because an abscess behind my kidney had been missed. Yet both were successful, and I was encouraged to walk a few steps the next day.

The absolute best I could have hoped was to still have enough good parts left to function without any medical appliance. I was grateful.

Recovery was different though. At 59, I fully expected that my healing might take longer than before. I was, however, determined to return to work. I was not going to retire due to illness.

After 11 days I was allowed to go home from the hospital, which was awesome, but I was still so weak. I spent my nights in bed and my days on the couch. My body still wore staples, like a railroad track down my abdomen, and there was still a drain that dangled from my right lower back that required daily care. My husband became a loving but reluctant nurse to support my care.

My brain was still foggy for weeks, likely from all the anesthetic, antibiotics, and pain meds received in the hospital as well as the surgery itself being a shock to my body. Even though all I could do was rest, I had difficulty reading or writing because I could not focus. So, I colored, five minutes at a time, with a big book of designs and colored pencils. It only took a tiny bit of concentration to color within the lines. By the end of the week, I had completed a picture.

Slow steps forward. I walked, first it was only down the stairs in the morning from the bedroom to the living room, back and forth to the washroom, and then back up the stairs at night. As my brain fog started to clear, I would challenge myself to make an extra trip along the hallway after walking to the washroom, and then another trip and then another until I was walking hundreds of steps a day that built to a thousand and then two thousand. Building up my stamina and strength so that by spring I was walking in the park daily for half an hour.

Besides wearing down the hallway carpet with pacing, I had hours to spend in thought while lying on the couch. I continued to visualize my inner body healing incisions and washing away inflammation. I was getting better and stronger. I was healing. But I had done the same for the first operation and yet the disease returned with a vengeance. What if it keeps to this pattern and returns in 30 years when I am 90? Could I, would I survive another surgery?

Of course, I now had a specialist who was prescribing biologic and wonder meds, to calm my overactive immune system from attacking my gut, with the goal of preventing further surgery. However, I wanted to be doing something. I needed to be a part of my healing and staying well. So, the more I colored and walked and visualized, the more of my focus returned. I began to read everything I could about the basics of wellness and healing.

I learned that given the right conditions, the human body will heal itself, find its balance, its homeostasis. I had been seeing this all my life with cut fingers and scrapped knees that healed. All the cells in the body can heal in the same way. I had just not thought about it in that way.

It was my fork in the road, my definitive moment when I realized that the possibility existed that it was in my power to support my own health and avoid further surgery. But many things in my lifestyle and career routine would have to change to sustain the wellness I was building.

I began by drinking more water and stopped drinking soda pop. More whole foods, fruits and vegetables, and less processed foods became part of our meals. Sleep, a full seven to eight hours of complete sleep nightly was now imperative. It also meant adding a condition for returning to work that traveling would need to be reduced so that my body would not suffer sleep deprivation from frequent time zone adjustments in a month. I continued to maintain my walking schedule. Yet with all my research on healing, I still had one more hurdle to embrace to create balanced well-being. It was something I had not ever tried, nor thought necessary.

However, the studies and authorities on the subject reported it to be key to linking the body, mind, and spirit together for holistic healing wellbeing. I was finally ready to find my connection to myself in the universe and began to learn to meditate. To get started, I told myself, it was to calm my nervous system to reduce the body's stress and inflammation. I started with short, guided meditations where there was a five minute preamble for setting an intention and then 10-15 minutes of mantra of focused meditation.

It was not easy. My thoughts have been known to disco dance around my brain when I try to settle into any focused activity, and it was no different with meditation. But it was ok. There was no need to panic. With a mantra I was able to notice the dancing thought distractions and came back to focus on the mantra.

After a few months of improved ability to focus on a mantra, my body and mind started feeling calm and untriggered by passing issues. I started enjoying longer meditation sessions and planned them almost daily to feel equanimity and whole. Meditation became a time when I was able to touch the center, my center of who I am, apart from my physical body. I could sense being expansive and connected to what felt like the entire universe. I was in awe that I had spent two thirds of my life without the experience of what I was learning and feeling through meditation.

I healed and recovered fully in 11 months and returned to full time work after 15 months to complete a major project to replace my company's computer system. My plan was to retire once the project was completed. However, the Universe had other plans and after a year and a half being back to work, the pandemic lockdown gave some of us, including me, the opportunity to retire early.

My health continues today using the techniques that empowered me to heal from my surgery and illness. I have learned that the challenges or bumps in the road made my life's journey not only just about the struggle through to healing but also provided me the opportunity for a rich personal growth experience.

Life is meant to be an adventure. Take the time to let wounds heal first, then seek what lessons there are to be learned and what growth can be gained looking back from the perspective of a scar. Where I once avoided a glance, I now fondly view my scars as visible reminders of my resilience. Evidence that I am empowered to impact my own wellness and that it is my responsibility to pick myself up when I stumble and bounce back to try again. It gives me the confidence to face the unknown and feel that in the end, the adventure will turn out alright.

I now teach others who, like me, may be unaware that wellbeing is an inside job that we have the ability and power to direct. My full intention going forward is to first, enjoy these best last 30 plus years of my adventure, with a healthy and resilient wellbeing. And second, to assist as many other women as possible, who are interested, to be empowered also by their own wellbeing.

Who else wants to cultivate their health and resilience, heal their life's wounds into scars of gratitude, and is not yet ready for a rocking chair?

Sabrina Lambert

...

Alice Walker

"Time moves slowly, but passes quickly."

9

Obstacles
ENDLESS AND IMPOSSIBLE TO CONQUERED

"Yourself and all that you are. Know that there is something inside you that is greater than any obstacle." - Christian Larson

Have you ever experienced grief so deeply that you clutched your heart and dropped to your knees because the physical pain in your heart was so intense you could do nothing else? I have.

I was on a run to clear my thoughts, breathe fresh air and soak in the sunshine; to heal. My mind was weary and wanted permission to pause; however, grief now occupied every cell in my body. Thoughts flooded in, dominating, and I began to cry as my legs continued to run. Thoughts of the husband and two very young boys my best friend left behind in her passing from melanoma. Thoughts of the empty space in my heart that was created when she left and will remain forever empty as no one could ever be that caliber of a friend to me.

As I knelt in a ditch on the side of a neighborhood road, clutching my shattered heart, and sobbing, I realized how powerful my thoughts were and how deep the levels of grief run. I knew the intense pain felt was from my broken heart. My best friend's passing at age 34, my years of infertility, three natural miscarriages, and my seven-year-old niece suffering a brainstem stroke had taken their toll.

So much grief occupied my heart and soul, yet simultaneously much gratitude filled the same space. I was on this daily intense roller-coaster ride of emotions, trying to process the death of my best girl-friend, the death of our miscarried babies, the unclear future of our infertility journey, and the uncertainty of our sweet niece's brain-stem stroke. Yet, in the deep thought channels of grief also flowed a river of gratitude.

I was incredibly grateful I was solid in my faith. I had an amazing, optimistic husband, supportive family on both sides, and a solid network of special friends from grade school, plus new friends made since moving to Kansas City after marriage. My mind constantly fluctuated between deep levels of grief never experi-enced before, and pure gratitude for all God had provided me in this life. It was intense grief blanketed with intense love. It was a lot.

I spent many nights at the Children's hospital caring for my niece, so my sister could at least try and sleep to tackle the daytime chaos of doctor rounds, brain scans, my niece's waxing, and waning, and her in and out of her ICU. I worked full-time as a Registered Clin-ical Dietitian at a different hospital. I would stay the night with my niece as we never wanted her to be alone and in the am shower, get ready for work, eat at the hospital, then drive directly to my work. I worked in the oncology unit, and during the intense period of my niece's recovery, three of my favorite patients entered the unit within months of each other not returning home again—more deaths to process.

As the days blurred into one another, it became increasingly diffi-cult to balance it all. The obstacles to overcome seemed endless and impossible. Because I have never been in such an over-whelming emotional place, I never realized I was an emotional eater. I began to eat for comfort and gained fifteen pounds in the process. As a Registered Dietitian educated to eat for health and trained to maintain a healthy weight, this was a considerable amount of weight to gain. And for a period of time, it helped me cope with my issues until the day it didn't. I recall teaching a Cardiac Rehab class at the hospital with an exercise physiologist. I remember standing in front of a group of patients who had recently experienced a heart attack, teaching them how to eat to best support their hearts and how to reduce weight to reduce the workload of their hearts. Me, standing there teaching while carrying an extra fifteen pounds.

I felt like a complete imposter. Why would they listen to me when it was clearly visible, I was not presenting as an individual in optimal health. Being healthy and looking healthy is an unwritten expecta-tion of a Registered Dietitian. Why would they believe anything I had to say? How could I explain all that was happening to me, and more importantly, how could I truthfully rationalize my comfort eating? I could not.

These patients deserved to receive the best knowledge and guidance I had to offer. I needed to deliver the information in a manner that reflected my authentic self. It did not matter what was going on in my personal journey. They deserved the best of me. They were there to learn cutting-edge nutrition education so they could move forward in their journey. My concerns were not their concerns. Another obstacle. I knew I had to get myself in top shape for them and tackle my newfound comfort eating head-on. I began to run again.

I thought a lot as I ran; I thought a lot all the time. Thoughts constantly raced, occasionally slowing their pace but never enough for me to catch relief. The grief catapulted me to a different level without my permission. I felt I was not on the same cosmic plane as others. I recall people speaking about mundane subjects, and it was very hard for me to focus on the words. It took a considerable amount of energy to listen, and I did listen partly because of genuine interest and partly to escape my thoughts.

If the words turned negative at any point, I found myself shutting down and immediately tuning out their words because I simply could not relate. I would look directly into the person's eyes and think, how could their frustration of poor service in a restaurant, a challenging patient, or an uncooperative colleague compare? Couldn't they see or understand how devastated I felt? I was right in front of them, yet I felt unseen.

The communication gap was wide, even with family and close friends. I noticed how quickly others forgot the challenges I faced in my daily struggles. I noticed how soon I was expected to "be myself." Their interpretation of what they needed me to be surfaced loud and clear. I knew in my heart they meant well. I understood they did not comprehend this level of grief. They did not yet grasp the "me" they knew and loved was no longer. She was gone- forever. It would take time for them to connect and realize this new reality.

My husband Andy and I would take breaks between the intense fertility treatments and failed cycles. We would celebrate "us" and all the wonderful relationships we shared with our families and friends. We celebrated our successes at work and the freedom we had to play golf after work and/or go to a movie and dinner as we chose. We were grateful for those easy, relaxed times and grateful we had each other. We made a great team and were best friends as husband and wife. Although we were on breaks from treatments, we never truly were on a break from our thoughts. Thoughts: Will we ever be the parents we longed to be or is our next treatment cycle the one that makes us parents? Why is all this happening to us? Are we crazy for trying again? These were thoughts that lingered whether we were on breaks or not and weighed heavily. It was nice, though; we remained consistent in the rhythm of breaks and treatments. When one was ready to try again, the other was right by his/her side, ready for the challenge. There were not long, intense discussions of should we, shouldn't we.

When one announced they were ready, we both dove in. I can tell you, with absolute truth, that there is nothing natural or spontaneous about fertility treatments. Once treatments begin, so does the intensity. Protocols are precisely outlined, and everything is timed and calculated with very narrow time windows. You are in constant contact with the physician or nurses. Medications are ordered, needles and alcohol swabs are delivered, and ultrasounds are scheduled. It became a daily part-time job keeping up with it all. I knew more about my body and the female cycle than I ever wanted to know. One becomes an expert going through fertility treatments. An expert you did not anticipate ever becoming.

Andy and I had the additional challenge of our fertility clinic being in a different city, 3.5 hours away. I recall always scheduling my ultrasounds as the last time slot of 9:30 am. I would leave Kansas City no later than 6:00 am and walk off the elevator into the clinic right around 9:30 am. Always greeted with "How was your drive?" "Smooth" was my consistent response because it was smooth, and I was most grateful for the uneventful drives. Each drive halfway through, I would pull to the side of the highway, reach for my insulated kit, draw up medication into a 1.5-inch needle and inject the needle into the large muscle on the top of my leg. I would need to alternate legs for each injection.

The good thing about a tight time schedule is I did not have time to wince or procrastinate. I gave myself a quick pep talk stating, "This is for us!" I would then inject, put the needle safely back, walk back and forth the length of the car a few times so as not to cramp, hop back in and pull back on the highway. After my ultrasounds, I would head back to my car and drive straight through to the hospital, where a full patient case load awaited my attention. I admit ultrasound days were long physically and mentally. The drives were mentally grueling because I was trapped in the car with my thoughts as unwelcomed passengers.

Another unanticipated experience going through fertility treatments is the constant reminders you have not yet achieved your dream of becoming parents. It appeared at times everywhere I turned. I would bump up against a pregnant momma. In the grocery store, the dentist's office, and the bank. I would even run on different days at different times and, without fail, pass by a beaming mom with a stroller.

Each time the mom would be walking so proud and look at me as if to say, "Look at my beautiful baby. "I could never muster the strength to stop and look. I would spot the beaming mom from a distance and feel my heart sink again. It was all I could do to smile as I passed her, holding back tears as I continued to run. Then on top of the sadness came guilt. Guilt that I didn't stop to admire the newborn. Guilt that I didn't share in the sweet momma's happiness. I wanted to. However, profound grief was in the driver's seat. Thoughts fluctuated between guilt and grief for the remainder of the run.

One time on a down day, I recall being relieved to plop into our favorite movie theater seats only to have a pregnant momma sit down right next to me. I could typically handle this and, at times, not think twice about it; however, there are days in one's infertility journey when the absence is so great you are as fragile as a snowflake.

That evening, grief won as we surrendered our favorite seats. Fielding the random questions and statements also became challenging, especially after our miscarriages. I would be inclined to answer questions of all sorts, such as when will you and Andy start a family? Have you thought about having kids? There is nothing wrong if you and Andy decide you do not want kids. Not want kids…. if only they knew.

Of course, my best friend knew. Andy and I were a couple of years into our infertility journey when she became ill. Missy was amazing in the fact she did not want to focus on her illness ever during our conversations, so she would always ask how things were going.

One particular conversation will forever be in my memory bank. Andy and I were perplexed as to why we were struggling so. It was always in our plans to have children. We wanted three children, with the first born being a boy to protect his sister and other brother. We wanted them close in age as Andy came from a family of four boys, each two years apart, and they were great friends growing up. We both knew we wanted to be parents and believed we would be parents. It was a matter of when and how.

We had many discussions and considered all options. I was beginning to wonder if our plan included adoption, so I signed up for an adoption seminar held at a local hospital. Andy was traveling at the time, so I decided to gather the information to report back. Missy and I were in conversation later that week. I brought up adoption as a consideration. Missy instantly responded with clarity and sheer confidence, "That is NOT God's plan for you. "She didn't elaborate and sat in silence on the other line. It stunned me a bit, and from that moment on, I never had the inkling to pursue the subject any further. Message received.

Missy and I often had rich, deep conversations even prior to her becoming ill. We rarely gossiped because it was not something either of us enjoyed. We enjoyed telling each other funny stories of our mishaps of the day, and we always talked about the day she and her husband would move to Kansas City after raising our families. We made plans to live by each other, sit in rocking chairs on wraparound porches and grow old together. A dream that would stay a dream.

Days turned into weeks, and weeks turned into long months. I felt stagnant, weary and a bit lost. I was at work when I received word Missy's condition turned. Andy and I had travel plans to attend his work convention in Hawaii. Travel plans obviously were canceled; instead, I traveled to St. Louis on a train to see my best friend, who now spent her days in the ICU unit, knowing this would be the last time I would see her breathing. Andy was to meet me in St. Louis later when funeral arrangements were made. Here again, I found myself in intense grief wrapped in a blanket of pure love and gratitude.

Pure love for my dying friend and grateful beyond measure I had time off to spend with her and her family. I entered the ICU late evening and was stopped by her nurse. I'm sorry, only family is allowed to see her now. Without hesitation and slowing my pace, I looked directly into the nurse's eyes and said I am family; I am her sister. And I remember meaning those words with all my heart. We were that close; she was my sister.

As I entered her room and gently called her name, her eyes met mine briefly, and I knew she knew it was me visiting. Her eyes remained closed for the remainder of our visit, and I certainly didn't mind because I knew she heard my voice and all my words. I held her hand and told her how much I loved her and that I would miss her terribly. I reminisced aloud all our fun and wonderful times. I told her what an incredible friend she had been to me and that no friend would ever take her place. Then we sat in silence for a very long time.

The next day the decision was made for comfort care, and she was moved to a private room to make her transition. The family was told it would be any time now. When I arrived, her bed was surrounded by family and friends.... standing room only. I learned she had not opened her eyes for two weeks prior to my visit. What a gift she gave me. Pure gratitude filled my heart.

I shared a bit of Missy and my visit with my other friends, and each of them said how lucky I was to have said my goodbyes in private. So many filled her room constantly. The nurses finally told her husband to have everyone leave so she could make her transition.

They explained when there are so many gathered, it is hard for the soul to depart because they are torn between staying and leaving.

Sure enough, when her room was finally empty, she stayed with her husband a bit longer and exited in the early morning of October 22nd. Interestingly, Missy's birthday was 1-22, her first born son's birthday 2-22, her second son's birthday 3-22, and she made her transition on 10-22. She knew what she was doing and when she wanted to leave this earth.

Processing all I was experiencing during this period of my life became a challenge, and it was getting harder and harder to manage. The waves of grief pounded closer and closer together and became harder to predict. I kept a heart medallion on my keychain as a reminder of the close friendship Missy, and I shared. I wanted something visible to carry to keep her memory by me throughout my days.

I was checking out at the local pharmacy when the pharmacist made a comment about how much she liked the heart on my keychain. I smiled. She kindly asked about its significance; the only words registered in my mind were the remembrance of my dead friend. I couldn't speak and began to cry. All I could do was mumble an apology, grab my prescription and run out of the store. This was the first time I was unable to compose myself and control the grief. I was stunned, embarrassed and my heart hurt. Grief is funny like that. You think you are in control and doing well considering your circumstances, then boom, an unexpected trigger followed by an unmanageable flood of tears appears without warning.

Dealing with grief started to consume more time than I was willing to devote. I was growing weary and frustrated. I missed me; I missed happy me. Life changed me, and maintaining a positive outlook became exhausting. I was definitely lost and began to doubt my faith for the first time.

I recall announcing to my husband I planned to take a break from attending church because after analyzing all that had happened, I could no longer see the benefit. I was devoted to my faith, and my world continued to crumble around me. What was the point of it all became the question for me. I remember Andy's direct response stating it was not a suitable solution. He asked me to continue even though it may not seem like it is helping at the moment. He continued to point out that my faith had always been a center for me and would eventually prove so in this season. I was reluctant but agreed more out of respect for his request verses wanting to attend.

Truthfully, anger began sneaking in and taking over grief. I decided I wanted space and distance from God. So that is what I did. My heart was wounded, my soul beyond weary. I went to church but was not present. My conversations with God became very different. I told him I had enough. I was very hurt and frustrated and really did not want much to do with him. Surprisingly, I did not feel bad or guilty about this communication. I stated my feelings and plan to deal with it all by myself. I knew turning my back completely on God was unwise and not something my heart ever considered. However, I decided I no longer had the energy to devote to my faith. It was all I could do to get through the life responsibilities of a day.

One day, I was gazing out the window and had a vision of Jesus sitting on a white fence in the distance. He was just sitting there in his robe, his sandals resting on one of the lower bars of the fence. I told him I could see him and asked him to stay where he was in the distance and to not move even an inch toward me. I found it comforting to see him but still wanted nothing further to do with him. This vision stayed clear for several months. I remember thinking, ok, good, I can still see you, and perfect, you have not moved closer.

To be honest, I subtly expected Jesus to move closer each time I saw the vision. He never did. I began to ponder why. I still could not bring myself to ask him to move closer, nor did I want to move toward him. We remained at a standstill. I began to grow tired of the pondering. Just another obstacle I did not want to tackle. So that is how the vision stayed for quite a while. At some point, I decided this vision of communication as it was no longer served me.

I was slowly beginning to heal and realized although it was good to see God in the distance, it would be better if he were closer, and it would be best to close the gap for good. Unexpectedly, I found this to be very difficult. I froze and didn't know how to proceed forward. I made an appointment with a priest at the church I attended. Maybe he could help. I told the priest my story, all of it, and asked him for his thoughts regarding ways to move closer to God while grief was still raw.

His response was quite helpful and gave me the confidence to remain steady and solid in my faith throughout the years that followed. He explained the level of grief I was experiencing was far from normal for someone in their thirties. That level of grief is typically not experienced until people reach their sixties. He continued by saying, for whatever reason, God had me experience this level of grief during my thirties. He told me not to question it and instead to be grateful because the wisdom I would gain from this period of time will serve me well. It was exactly what I needed to hear.

Confirmation my life experiences thus far were indeed intense for my age and that my rollercoaster of emotions were valid. He also suggested I be the one to move to close the gap between Jesus and me. He suggested I move toward him a little each day. He said even if some days you move only a ½ inch, it's ok. It is a move in the right direction, and as long as I kept moving each day, the communication gap would eventually close.

This time relief flooded over me, and as time went on, the anger, grief, frustration, and guilt once felt dissipated, and the gap did close. I now felt the strength to overcome any and all obstacles. My faith strengthened, and my communication with God improved exponentially. I asked many questions all the time, and inevitably answers would come in many different forms and ways. Answers always appeared; it was something I learned to trust and count on.

If the obstacles in your life seem endless and impossible, know the solutions lie within your heart. There are reasons behind each struggle and with each struggle comes incredible growth. Ask the questions and trust the responses delivered to you. Answers always come. You are never alone in your struggles, nor do you have to solve anything all by yourself. Help surrounds you; just ask the questions and trust with every fiber of your being.

I am eternally grateful I did, and because I did, I now get to share the lessons learned with our boy/girl twins.

Dana Cartwright

...

Alison Croggon

"There are many futures and many pasts, and your present is but a
tiny fulcrum, changing all of them..."

10

Someday I'll Be Okay - But Someday Never Comes
IT'S NOT A DATE ON THE CALENDAR

"The stories we tell ourselves shape our lives. They shape who we believe we are, and this belief translates into who we become."
- John Assaraf

I used to be skinny, painfully thin as a young child, and well into young adulthood. I was teased, kidded, bullied, and made fun of because of it. I was very shy as a child, and my weight issues felt very isolating as I looked to others around me – who didn't struggle with being skinny. If anything, their struggle was the opposite – very different from mine. I felt very alone and isolated. As a result, I often felt different, out of place and misunderstood.

Growing up as the oldest child in a family of six children made it hard to be noticed. There were just so many voices in the chaos. And a value that was expressed often in our home that I took into my young, tender heart – was "Children should be seen, and not heard."

And so, the belief or story I told myself rather early in my formative years was that my feelings or point of view didn't matter. Everyone else came first and was more important in the scheme of things.

And this was reinforced when my parents looked to me as the oldest to watch over my younger siblings when they occasionally went out for the evening.

I remember being very anxious when they were gone. Because I felt so responsible for my siblings. I lived with much fear that something would happen to one of them "during my watch." And I couldn't bear being a disappointment to my parents or not have them be pleased with my performance as their trusted caretaker. I was born a "people pleaser," and pleasing people for love and acceptance was something I perfected over the course of my life.

So as a young child not much older than my siblings, I took on the responsibility of tending to their needs and became a worried, anxious young adult, with seemingly no voice to express it. I grew up feeling that I was loved conditionally – in other words, when I did what pleased, when I was good, when I was obedient.

I never felt loved just for who I was, or just because I existed. And again, because there were so many voices that seemed to require attention, and I obediently was silent as expected, I rarely heard – much less felt -- that my folks were proud of me for who I was vs what I did.

And so began my life-long journey to put myself second, to strive hard to please, to go above and beyond, and to do good things so that I would FEEL the love for me in what I did or in my performance. This led to the belief that if I just DID enough good, that it would lead to the love and acceptance I craved so much. This all led to self-esteem issues – which also impacted my confidence and trust in myself as I moved forward in my life. I struggled with low self-esteem and confidence issues for a good portion of my life.

Now I want you to understand, my parents were good parents who just happened to have lots of kids. The oldest three – were all two years apart, and then the other three were spaced out over the course of several years. They came along five years, then 18 months, and finally 11 years later. So, it seemed like there were always babies in the house, and their needs were immediate – not necessarily more important. But again, I felt I should take a back seat to all the other needs going on in a very busy household.

And so, the story or beliefs I told myself in my youth took over. I was not important enough or maybe just not loud enough to be heard in the noise and chaos. And my brain did what our brains do. I looked for evidence to support this story or belief as I continued into adulthood. And so, on a subconscious level, I continued to form the belief or told myself the story that I wasn't enough. I needed to perform my way to love and acceptance.

It is from that point of reference that I want to share two stories from something that happened in my childhood/young adulthood. I want to give you some insight into how something that doesn't seem to be such a big deal at the time can impact us for a lifetime. And it often happens without our even realizing it because of the stories we tell ourselves and how it shapes our beliefs. You will see in these two examples, how my brain was seeking evidence that my story – or belief, supported what I believed.

When I was young, my dad often introduced me to others like this. And note, it was with a great deal of pride. He said, "This is my oldest daughter, Linda. She's a little thin now, but she'll fill out."

Now, as I look back, I'm certain he didn't mean for these words to make me feel badly about myself. Remember, he introduced me with love and pride. However, I took time much later in my life to revisit some of my limiting beliefs -- those old stories we tell ourselves that we believe to be true but are not. I took this to mean I'm not Okay now, but SOMEDAY I will be.

And guess what? Someday never comes. I moved forward into adulthood with the belief, or story that I told myself that I wasn't enough – that I'd be okay if I just kept trying to please. That it would come eventually, someday, with practice. And thus began my constant striving to please – to keep going forward to Someday. That day that doesn't exist on the calendar that is so elusive. And so, going forward in my career life, I was continually striving to be successful someday, and to do more to be "enough" and valued for who I would BE Someday.

Now those words from my dad hurt for a long time. It was even difficult to tell it without getting emotional for a good part of my life. Because you see – those seemingly unintentional comments weren't said to hurt me. But they came from someone I really loved. Someone who I tried desperately to please. And if he didn't like the me that was before him – how and why would someone who didn't know me feel?

As a result, I grew up thinking and feeling that if people knew the real me, they wouldn't like what they saw. After all, my dad (who knew me better than most) didn't like the me before him - that awkward, skinny, lacking in self-esteem little girl, why would anyone else? I grew up subconsciously thinking, that there must be something inherently wrong with me. This was another belief or story I worked on for a good part of my life. It was especially apparent when I would ultimately come up against unknowing comments of what felt like disapproval or criticism or worse rejection. It affirmed and added to the evidence that I was collecting that I was not okay as I was. But I held on to the hope of "Someday."

Another story to illustrate how I built up evidence of this belief or story I was telling myself occurred when I was a senior in high school. I was thinking about and planning for my future career. As a first-born child and people pleaser, I was a very good student. I was dutiful, obedient, and quiet. I did what I could to get good grades to prove that I was good enough and pleasing to my parents and teachers.

As I talked with my parents about wanting to go to college, my dad said to me – again lovingly, "I don't have any money for YOU to go to college. I saved money for your brothers. You're just going to meet someone who will take care of you."

Again, I collected more evidence of my story or belief that girls aren't important and took this to mean girls don't have the same value as men. Their opinions don't matter. It worked best to be seen, not heard. Their purpose is taking care of men and families. This was more evidence that I wasn't good enough, my voice wasn't important, and therefore I needed to keep on striving to do what pleased.

Please note, that raising children and taking care of families are important purposes. I don't want anyone to downplay that or think that I don't know its value. Raising responsible adults that positively impact society, may be the most important job there is. However, with my upbringing and always needing to do more and be more, I thought that was what I needed to do to be the best mom for my son.

As you may have determined from these two examples, I may have some daddy/authority issues too. I wrapped up a lot of negative feelings about men in authority over women. That also didn't serve me so well in my career. Until I went back and, in effect, rewrote or reframed that story to be more effective and empowering to serve me better in my life going forward.

The more empowering story I tell myself now is this. I owe my dad a debt of gratitude for his shaping me into the person I am today. What he intended to DISCOURAGE me – drove me toward getting my degree completed, almost in spite of him. And now, out of his six children, I am the only one who graduated and has a four-year degree.

The completion of that degree opened many doors for me as I made my way into the world of work. And left to myself, I may have given up were it not for that determination and will to please my dad that kept me going to get it done. It also was a matter of integrity for me, and I wanted to be a woman of my word. I wanted to show my dad that I could do it. And you know what? No one was prouder of me than he was for my being the first to go to college and complete a degree. And the really surprising thing? I was proud of me too! I was beginning to show myself that I was capable of achieving great things – "someday."

So, you see, I am making progress. I have gone back to those days, and have, in effect, rewritten it to form a new belief or a new story. I tell myself something that serves me better and is more empowering. "I may not be there yet, but in the meantime, I can always improve and be better." "I gain confidence by taking action and learning from all my experiences – good and bad – and can take those lessons forward as I improve." "I can toss the experience but keep the lesson." "With each baby step of action I take, I continue to develop confidence and belief in myself."

And now I can talk about it without tearing up in an inspiring, positive way. You see, I discovered that our tears are often a signal that we haven't fully dealt with what's underneath, and that more healing needs to take place. And that what lies beneath the emotional pain might point to something that is preventing us from moving forward – a place of resistance or a limiting belief in ourselves that is keeping us from being all we were created to be.

And often, which has been true for me, we need someone outside of the experience to help us make sense of it or be willing to do that deep internal work of really discovering what is holding us back. And many aren't willing to revisit those painful places, thinking they've dealt with it, and really haven't.

I know I had been guilty of that until I came to the realization over time that I was not reaching my full potential due to the belief that I would be good "someday." Those beliefs, or old stories I was telling myself – were keeping me from being the best version of myself. These learnings have been a process. Questioning what has been holding me back at different points in my life. And continuing to strive to perform at my best and learn the lessons along the way.

After graduating from college with a degree in business education, I entered the workforce with some pretty shaky confidence skills. But my dogged determination to please actually came in handy! I just kept doing – performing at my best level – and eventually, I was noticed for what I did! But I still had some work to do to feel that confidence and belief I had anchored to "someday."

Although outwardly, what I showed of myself to those outside of me seemed like I was an accomplished, confident woman – INSIDE – I was anything but! I struggled with confidence in a huge way. My success came from just being so determined to show everyone that I could do it. Little did I realize, that along the way in my journey, I was showing myself too. It was those actions I took over time that helped my confidence grow. Until I FELT it too. But it was a process that took some time and a lot of introspection to get there.

And as is true for all of us, those limiting beliefs and old stories I told myself made an appearance throughout my life. Actually, they still show up. They show up as self-doubt, fear, lack of belief, fear of criticism, fear of being rejected, fear of failure – and even fear of success. But I recognize it sooner and tell myself more empowering thoughts as soon as I catch myself. Because awareness is the key. We can't fix what we don't acknowledge is broken.

My growing up years and taking care of my siblings led me to the teaching profession as my first job. I was always better at tending to others' needs ahead of my own, and teaching students affirmed these skills. I loved focusing on them and watching them grow in confidence as I encouraged them and breathed belief into them. Something I didn't do for myself early on in my career, brought me so much fulfillment in working with my students.

I ended up in human resources for most of my career. My experiences included everything from employment, career counseling, supervisory training, and eventually consulting work. Once again, a perfect fit as I could focus on others, and my needs could be secondary. As I reflect on it today, I think choosing this field allowed me to feel safe. I only needed to share bits of myself because everything and everyone I dealt with had to be held in strict confidence and the focus needed to be on those I served. There was comfort and safety in that. I was blessed and privileged to be trusted as they shared, and I needed to trust myself too – to find my authentic self to fully be all I was created to be.

In human resources, I didn't have to risk being vulnerable or share much of myself, thereby risking judgment, disapproval, or rejection throughout most of my career. My job was to listen to others and help them resolve personnel issues. I could use my silent, unassuming observing skills to listen and learn from others. And I was blessed to be able to fully utilize one of my gifts – the gift of encouragement. As I listened to their stories, I began to learn more about myself and my story too.

When I was in my 40s, I attended a life-changing bible study where I learned for the first time about the love God had for me. For me – His precious child. He loved me so much, He was willing to go to the cross for ME. It was life changing.

You see, I was raised in a church that did a great job of talking about the fear of God, but I missed most of the message on the love of God. We weren't discouraged from reading the bible on our own but didn't particularly feel encouraged either. So, for the first time in my life, I purchased my own bible and immersed myself (being the people pleaser and good student that I was!) in studying this God who created me in His image and loved and valued me so much.

I learned about His unconditional love for me, just because I was His child. It wasn't dependent on ANYTHING I did! That was a pretty foreign concept to this people pleaser – so I began the process of rethinking or reframing the story I had been telling myself. Obviously, this took a great deal of time. I still struggled at this point in my life with that nagging belief that people wouldn't like the real, authentic me until "Someday" when I could do enough good to deserve it.

Opening myself up to a new perspective, a new way to look at myself, brought on a renewed, more appreciated me. Perhaps "someday" was here – or at least it was closer than it had appeared to be so long ago.

I began to realize that as a people pleaser, I was trying hard to please everyone but me. I hadn't embraced my inner, authentic self. That awkward little girl was becoming the confident woman I always wanted to be. I was out of alignment with who I authentically was because I didn't fully love her – like God does. He loves me without judgment and with lots of grace! I needed to be more confident and believe in myself more, not for any one person, but for myself.

And perhaps, most importantly, I learned that I was looking outside myself for affirmation and acceptance, for strength and confidence, when I eventually learned it comes from within me. And it was there all the time. Waiting to tap into. I was learning to trust my inner voice and my instincts. I began to appreciate that sacred place where the Holy Spirit resides, that has always – and will always continue to guide me to my best life. I no longer needed to wait for "Someday." It's here today!

Before you think I lived a beautiful life full of wisdom and prosperity from that day forward, I need to bring you back to my reality, and probably yours too! Those old stories continued to show up throughout my life. It still does! Because those old patterns – those old stories and beliefs – are deeply embedded, and it took work to look for evidence of the new story I wanted to tell myself.

And isn't life like that? We go along for a time where it flows. Then we bump into events, people, and situations that can take us back to old ways of thinking and being in a heartbeat. And it often leads us to a place where we need to ask questions, deep, thoughtful questions about our life and how we want it to be different.

So, fast forward a bit for a few more examples of what that lack of confidence, self-doubt, and people pleasing can lead to. It demonstrates what unhealed emotional pain can become.

Several years back, I went through a severe bout of depression that lasted several years. It was brought on by grief – a lot of losses (not just of persons) that I experienced in a short timeframe. The pain I felt the most was my only son leaving home for college. Truly my husband and I were as excited for him and his future as we were sad for ourselves in his next exciting chapter. And we discovered that we were way better at giving roots than wings! It was difficult to close this wonderful chapter of being his mom and dad and his being at home with us all the time.

In addition, I had lost a job, a couple of special people, and my role and identity as a mom and wage earner, to name just a few. I was in a negative place in my head due to fears and self-doubt, again! And so, the negative self-talk was playing in my head 24/7. I said things to myself that I would never say to another person.

It was suggested that I go see someone to help me through the emotional healing process. It was probably one of the first times that I truly bared my soul, and I found the experience so helpful. There was joy and freedom in the releasing of some of those old stories that continued to surface. And my counselor said that grief (loss) comes in many forms and just sits on our shoulders waiting to be dealt with. But it does need to be dealt with. And I learned that the practice of gratitude and journaling my thoughts were the best tools I could use for my healing. And it's a discipline I still do most days. There is power in getting our thoughts out of our head and onto paper.

So, although I wouldn't want someone to learn these lessons through depression, I remind myself often to toss the experience, but keep the lesson in moving through the challenges life brings. Because I took time to explore my emotions and what my inner self was teaching me, I learned to give myself the grace and compassion I so easily and willingly give to others. I learned to be my own best friend. And I grew deeper spiritually by learning to trust God – and ultimately myself – for the answers that were deep within me.

A more recent outcome of people pleasing and putting myself second led to a physical response versus the mental, emotional response of depression. I took on the role of leadership in a faith-based spiritual movement during a time when the organization was going through some particularly challenging times. In my attempt to please everyone except myself and get things done, I literally ran myself into a health scare.

I neglected my self-care. I took care of everyone else but myself. I re-engaged with unhealthy eating habits and overeating to cope with the stress and disapproval of some in the organization who either didn't like or didn't want to change in the direction we had to go if we were to survive.

I was under a great deal of stress, which I thought I was managing well – but my body was not in agreement. I ended up with A-fib and congestive heart failure from neglecting to take care of myself for so long and pushing myself too far.

However, this was not only a wake-up call for me -- it was actually a blessing in disguise. I took time to pause and reflect as I took a more in-depth inner journey and found my true authentic inner voice. Because I was in the "close to retirement" phase in my life, I asked myself questions I never found the time to ask in those busy mom years of running a household, raising my boy, and being a partner in a consulting business.

What are my gifts? What is my purpose? What is it I really want from my life in the time remaining? What impact do I want to make on the world? Big Questions! They required finding my center, my values, and my priorities and create a way to live my very best life with the best version of myself. You see, God was calling me higher. He loved me just as I am – but loved me enough to want more from me, and so He didn't let me stay here.

In this time of a forced pause of sorts, I learned a lot of lessons that I took forward with me. I learned that I could re-write my old stories to serve me better. I'd always believed in honest communications with others, and I needed to be honest with myself, too.

I learned to make time for taking good care of my mind, body, and spirit and learned how interconnected they are. I learned to trust my inner voice even more – to take my own advice that I often give to others. I learned once again that the answers to those deep questions lie within me and that I could trust my intuition. I needed to celebrate myself more, especially the small daily actions I took toward the life I wanted. I now spend time daily in quiet and gratitude to set each day off with positive intentions. And I serve others from a place of love for myself – and embracing my value – which makes my relationships so much richer. I learned FINALLY that Someday is here! It's now. It's right where I am!

So how about you?

Are YOU holding on to some "old stories?" Are you open to rewriting those chapters in your life's book to serve you better? What might happen when you decide to let an old story go? Once you've identified an old story in your life that is no longer serving you – you're able to begin to believe in a more authentic YOU. Ask yourself, as you go on your inner journey, what would happen if you let it go and reframed it to serve you better?

In my case, it helped me increase my confidence and belief in myself. It made me feel that I had so much more potential to serve from than I had ever imagined. It allowed those little girl dreams to come true because I didn't let that inner lack of confidence derail me from the person I was becoming. It made me realize that my

"Someday" was now. I accepted what was – what is – and what will be is all part of God's amazing plan for my life.

Today this inner journey of discovery that I purposefully and intentionally took has become my current chapter. I listened to that inner voice and recently launched the Believe in YOU Academy, where I now guide others struggling with confidence/belief/mindset issues and bring them through a similar inner journey to their authentic selves. We work on reframing or rewriting those "old stories" to serve us better and take that newfound confidence and belief in themselves out to a world that needs their gifts.

They, too, are learning to trust that inner voice, and go after with clarity and confidence those things that bring joy, meaning, and purpose to life. They are writing some amazing future chapters as a result. It has affirmed in me the belief that we are not just human beings – we are human becomings!

Your "Someday" is now too. You deserve it! You just need to learn it for yourself, as stated in a quote from one of my favorite childhood movies – The Wizard of OZ.

"You've always had the power, my dear. You just had to learn it yourself."
Glenda, the Good Witch

Linda S. Nelson

...

Mother Teresa

"If you judge people, you have no time to love them."

11

Raising My Sons Twice

A STORY OF ULTIMATE LOVE

"To love unconditionally is to look for the gifts unveiled, even when fear blinds the heart and conceals our courage."- Rosa Livingstone

I knew I wanted children someday. Not a burning desire but a certainty. And I believed that choosing to have children meant that it was my responsibility to keep them safe, to teach them to be independent adults with self-assurance, to love them no matter what, and to 'fix' their boo-boos with Band-Aids and kisses. This was my Credo.

I was blessed with two Sons, seven and a half years apart. Andrew and Jordan, the lights of my heart.

When they came into my life, I believed the worst that could happen was a broken bone, some stitches from a fall (I had boys, after all), gastral flues, chicken pox, measles, runny noses, and fevers. And when I read or heard about real tragedies involving children, I'd shudder and think, "Thank goodness that's not my child".

There's a saying I've come to believe is true for me, from a spiritual sense: "Want to make God laugh? Tell Her your plan". And my plan didn't include what unfolded with my boys.

I want you to know, right from the start, that I believe my story as a mother didn't choose me.

I chose my story, long before I showed up here in physical form. I believe that we are all in this classroom called "Life" to remember many qualities; qualities we came into this life with that allows us the ability to feel, think and do, such as:

- Compassion
- Kindness
- Selflessness
- Courage
- Giving and receiving love

Life has a way of testing us by creating challenges that bring us to our knees. Why? Because when this happens, we have a choice. We can either choose to reach deep inside, beyond the murk of our fears, to find our "brave" and bring it to the light or remain doggy paddling tirelessly in the shadowy dark.

There have been many dips in my life but the experiences with my sons were the most heart-wrenching but with the greatest gifts. To love is to look for the good and this is what I choose every day.

If you've been with me so far, keep reading and I'll tell you why. And to do that, you need to know a bit about this story.

In 2005, my first foray into one of the most terrifying experiences of my life began with my son Jordan, who was 4 years old. He was quite suddenly diagnosed with a life-threatening brain tumor.

The second was in 2018 with my eldest son, Andrew, who at 24 was hit by a car while riding his motorcycle. Thrown 40 feet, he landed on his head. Even though he was wearing a very costly and highly rated helmet, he sustained a Severe Traumatic Brain Injury.

Two different sterile hospitals – one for children and one for adults 13 years between events

Yet, two sons with brain injuries that almost took their lives. Same smells. The same sounds of machines beeping. Same hushed, anxious voices. Same harsh commands over speakers calling "Code Blue". Same rush of activity by staff. Same frantic families, waiting or visiting their loved one, hoping for the best outcome.

Jordan began feeling sick on the Remembrance Day long weekend. Saturday afternoon he had been playing with his dad and brother when he ran to me to tell me he his head hurt and needed to "puke". Once he'd vomited, he felt fine.

But the next day it happened again, and I was starting to get concerned. What kind of flu was this???? He vomits and the headache goes away??? My gut was worried. I can't even tell you why I knew something was terribly wrong.

The Tuesday when I returned to work, I sat with my Sales Executive and told her about what happened with Jordan and said, "I think this is neurological". Of course, she thought I was over-reacting. I would, too, if I was her. Call it Mother's Instinct. I felt this intense fear in my stomach and made an appointment with our Family Physician to have him checked out that same day.

When his babysitter brought him to the medical office, I noticed a droop on the side of his bottom lip and wondered if he'd had a stroke. In my heart, I now just knew this was bad!

After an examination, our Family Doctor, who I trusted completely, said we should get him to BC Children's hospital right away. I told her that was my plan from the get-go. She called ahead.

After many hours of waiting, and then endless tests, ending with an X-ray late at night, it was confirmed. A brain tumor the size of a lemon in my Baby's little head! Hearing that diagnosis felt like cold water being poured into my veins. I'll never forget that feeling.

First came disbelief. Then the terror set it.

My first question was, "Will my baby live?" The answer was, "We're doing all we can to get his brain pressure down right away. It's a miracle he didn't have a stroke before now".

I walked back to where my exhausted little boy finally lay sleeping. I kissed his temple, put my hand on his head, and prayed. Without knowing it, I was sending love to his brain so it would stop swelling. I was suffocating with a lump in my throat, looking at my helpless baby, so small in a big bed under white sheets.

Later I ran out to the parking lot in the pouring rain, fell to my knees, crying and screaming till I was hoarse. I was terrified, angry, and overwhelmed. My life to this point had been tough. I'd had to fight for every good thing in my life. Stoicism was my middle name. I'd survived an abusive family life and sexual abuse as a child. But this? My baby boy? How could I survive losing him?

I didn't know if I could withstand whatever the outcome would be. I was in a toxic relationship with his father, money was tight, I had a demanding job and another son to consider...how would I do all of this?

But something in my heart pulled me up off the ground by my backbone. I couldn't kiss this boo-boo better, but I **could** do whatever had to be done to shelter him, love him, and advocate for him. Losing my baby was not a thought I was going to entertain. He would live!

I became his Warrior Mama. I consulted with the Neurosurgeon as I wanted to understand everything that was happening in-order-to make the best decision I could for Jordan's wellbeing.

I clearly recall my eldest, Andrew, who was 11 at the time, being brought to the hospital by his father, my Ex, the next morning. He ran to me, crying, and asked if his brother would die. I spoke from my instinct and told him Jordan wouldn't die and that he'd have many more times to harass him (had to bring in some lightness). Yet my heart was struggling to be strong.

Jordan did live through the danger of the first 12 hours. Three days later he had surgery to remove the tumor. And there were positives and negatives to this. The positives were that most of the tumor was excised. Not all because it was in a dangerous spot.

Another was that after an agonizing five day wait, we learned that the tumor was non-cancerous. I think I went weak in the knees when the Neurosurgeon told Jordan's dad and me. The negatives were that Jordan had a life-threatening stroke during surgery and it caused him left side paralysis and right-side vision blindness.

After two weeks in the Children's Hospital, we spent five weeks in a Rehabilitation Hospital. I was allowed to stay 24 hours a day. I remember walking the halls the first night and having an anxiety attack. I couldn't breathe. I felt cold yet sweaty. How was I going to navigate this transition? At BC Children's Hospital, I had help to support Jordan emotionally and physically. Now I would have to be more hands-on. It scared the crap out of me. What if I dropped him? What if he saw my fear?

I recall the second night. Jordan was restless and mewling in his sleep. I got into his bed with him, from my cot, trying to soothe him. What I realized was that he was crying in his sleep out of frustration, wanting to turn his body in sleep, but the left side was still paralyzed. I put my nose into the back of his curls, wrapped my arms around him, and silently bawled. I spent the night turning him when he needed to move.

The days became more "normal". I fed him, changed him, and took him for rides in his wheelchair outside the hospital when the weather cooperated. I gave him his medications, took him to his therapy sessions, and advocated for a Child Psychologist.

You see, all the emphasis was on his physical healing. But the first day he was able to attend the Hospital's pre-school, he withdrew into himself. He confessed he felt "bad in the wheelchair". He didn't understand the what had happened to him. I wasn't equipped to explain things to him in a way he'd understand. So, I asked for help and a lovely Doctor was assigned to Jordan.

It wasn't all bleak. He took his first steps in the Hospital pool with his amazing Physiotherapist. I think I did cartwheels on the deck! This was hope. Hope that he would regain some mobility so that he could have more independence. I chose to look for the good and celebrate.

We were finally able to bring Jordan home. Again, I was terrified. What if he fell out of his wheelchair? How was I going to manage taking him out into the world in it? How would he react at the pre-school where he used to run like a wild child, the complete social butterfly?

Jordan's father wasn't much help, so Jordan's care fell mostly to me. I had to lift him to move him in and out of his wheelchair. I equated it to having a 40 pound baby.

I had to spoon-feed, wash, and bathe him. I had to hold him on the toilet because his left-side paralysis made it impossible for him to balance himself, even with bars on the adapted toilet seat. Wiping his bum was tough on him at first. Even at four years old he had a sense of his personal dignity, and he was so embarrassed to have Mama wipe his bum. But we talked it through, on the toilet seat, eye to eye. He cried. I cried. We got through it.

Did I complain? Hell no! I didn't lose him, so any hardship was a blessing.

Thankfully, he was able to relearn to walk and gained his independence slowly. He never regained the use of his left hand, but he came to understand, through his Psychologist and I, that this was not an impediment. This was not going to be used as an excuse not to try new things. In our home, it wasn't an option. He became a kid again, but with limitations.

Unfortunately, at 7 years old, the tumor began to regrow, as we were told it likely would, at some point, but I'd hoped for more time – like when he'd be an adult. Well, time ran out. Even though the tumor was benign, the only way to stop the growth was with Chemotherapy.

What? I was going to allow them to drip poison into his body? I struggled with that, but my logic knew this was our only option. If we didn't stop it, he would have a stroke and possibly die. He was too young for Radiation Treatment. Another surgery could blind him or worse. Fifteen months of Chemo. Once a week for four weeks and one week off. I was wracked with anxiety each time I'd drive him. But Jordan never complained.

The chemo did stop the growth but didn't shrink the damn tumor much! That had been my wish, but the concoction given to Jordan was experimental for kids. On the upside, he barely experienced any nausea and kept his beautiful, curly black hair.

In 2010, it began to grow again! I was shocked! Again, too freaking soon!! How was I going to tell Jordan, who was now 10 years old and more mature, that he had to endure Chemotherapy again? He'd endured so much already.

After I'd exhausted second and third opinions, Chemo, once again, was the best one. But by now, I'm a single Mom and an Entrepreneur. This was going to be a momentous task to bear. But his dad and I chose to align for Jordan's sake. After heartbreaking talks with Jordan to help him understand what was happening, we began another journey, only this time, it was ugly.

Every week for four weeks then one week off. And it made him so sick. Although Jordan, again, was so brave, he developed Anticipatory Anxiety and I'd have to stop on the way to the Hospital so he could vomit. I had to stay behind my eyes, or I'd lose it.

I had to change his chemo dates to Fridays so he wouldn't miss school. So, every weekend, my little Hero spent it vomiting and sleeping. His brother and I rallied to keep his spirits up. It was tearing out my heart but if he could be courageous, so could I.

After eighteen months of chemotherapy, this time, the tumor disappeared. I'd put my "bullshit" flaps on from the very beginning when Jordan's Oncologist would tell me not to get my hopes up as statistically, the tumor would shrink but not be eradicated.

She obviously didn't know my faith in the outcome I wanted. She didn't know I was a Hypnotherapist working with Jordan while he slept, helping him imagine a big "digger" removing the tumor and then creating a swimming pool (his choice) in its place. And she didn't know my Jordan, who when I asked him what he felt, would tell me, "Mom, I know it's going to be gone this time". And he believed. So, we believed together.

Jordan is soon to be 21 years old. And although his vision is impaired, and he wears splints on both his left leg and hand (he never regained the use of his left hand), he is out there in the world! He graduated, has a great job he loves in the Film Industry, moved out a year ago to explore himself, and is now in a relationship with an amazing young woman.

On October 8, 2022, the police knocked on my door at 8 pm to tell me that my son, Andrew, was at St. Paul's Hospital in Vancouver, having been in an accident on his motorcycle.

Again, it was ice water in my veins. They wouldn't tell my husband, John, and me, how serious it was. One of the Officers said, "Just get there as quick as you can". They offered to escort us, but my Husband had a cool head and he told me to pack a bag and he'd drive. I hyperventilated all the way there.

To walk into a sterile and bright room to see my child/man on a table with tubes in places they shouldn't be, is shocking to say the least. Yet he looked like he was sleeping, with his beautiful long lashes touching his cheek.

I learned he almost died at the scene. He was holding on by a thread. I recall imagining surrounding him in white light to strengthen that thread.

He had an amazing team when he transferred to I.C.U. that night. The following morning, the Intensivist explained what was happening. The physical injuries would have to wait. He was in a coma and the first 72 hours were critical.

Again, I filtered out what scared me to death. I **chose** to believe he'd pull through. Whatever the consequences.

I sang and talked to him. His core group of five Besties from kindergarten surrounded him with their positive energy from the first day. I learned from this experience that Andrew was very loved and had already made such a big impact on others.

He pulled through. After nine days he opened his eyes but my Andrew "wasn't there" yet. I continued to stay by his side 12 plus hours every day. My husband created the space so that I could focus on Andrew. We divided and conquered. My work skid to a halt.

I soon learned that as an adult, the medical community was not very receptive to my involvement. But I was relentless. No one was making decisions for him without my understanding WHY!

Every morning for over two months, I drove an hour to be at Andrew's side by 6:45 am in order to ensure I made the Doctors' rounds. I'd take notes. What I didn't know I'd Google (thank goodness for that) and then insist on answers the next day. I think I just ground them down because I became a fixture and they started asking ME if I had questions, which I did. The more I knew, the better I could advocate for him.

Each night I left the hospital crying. Initially, I was terrified that he might die without me at his side. Eventually, it was the terror of him falling out of bed because he was unaware that he couldn't walk yet kept trying. It happened twice in one night. Liken it to having a toddler who is 6 foot 2 inches. Another hit to the head could be devastating.

After two months, Andrew began speaking but it was mostly gibberish. A quick cognitive test was to ask him the names of familiar people and things. When asked my name, he said I was "Jesus". That was good with me.

He couldn't walk on his own. With staff shortages, I was giving him showers, brushing his teeth, feeding and changing him. Let me say that at 150 pounds, it was a combination of gymnastics and weight-lifting to get him out of bed and into a wheelchair.

We moved to a Rehabilitation Hospital and stayed for two and a half months. My advocation for his needs continued.

I stopped thinking about "when" we'd leave the hospital and continued to focus on one day at a time. That had been the promise my wonderful husband and I made as we drove frantically to Andrew on the rainy night of his accident.

During his stay, I'd pack him up every weekend to bring him home. I had to learn to administer his medications and feed him through his Feeding Tube as well as how to sanitize it each time.

Like his little brother, Andrew had a sense of his privacy from the start when I cared for his physical needs. He was embarrassed I'd have to bathe him and change his diaper. But I'd do it in such a way that he'd feel somewhat in control. A facecloth over his private parts seemed to do the trick.

Coming home was terrifying. I was already exhausted, and the prospect of what life would be like at home was daunting. But somehow, I found a pocket of reserves I never knew I had. I became his therapy consultant, his full-time care-nurse, and chauffeur, all the while continuing to be his mom. So many needs that it kept me hopping all day while still keeping my home running.

Andrew was more alert, but his brain was still healing. I felt I was now mentally dealing with a stubborn 12-year-old in a 25-year-old's body.

My friends would ask me how I could be so strong and do all I did. This actually bothered me. What else was I supposed to do? This was my son, my Baby, and it was my job to do what needed to be done to help him get to the other side of this. Granted, it wasn't easy but worth it.

Today, although Andrew can't return to work, he is moving forward, mostly independently. I am so proud and grateful.

I promised I'd explain what the greatest gifts I've received from these experiences are. Although these experiences were painful and I'm still working through some left-over PTSS eye-twitching, there is good that comes from tragedy.

From my fun-loving Jordan:

In leaving my very hectic and non-compassionate corporate job to take care of him, and knowing I needed to have an income, I found the most amazing and fulfilling career as a Clinical Hypnotherapist.

His courage showed me that I, too, could find my backbone and face the world with an attitude of curiosity and strength versus fear

I realized that I was more intelligent and capable than I'd ever given myself credit for learning to trust that I had something to say, to give, and could make create my reality. I wrote my first book in 2016, which was no small feat for the woman who had been so afraid of being judged. I learned to listen to my instinct, to laugh more at myself, and find the beauty of each moment that were pregnant with possibility. I chose to keep looking for the positive instead of letting my fearful monkey-mind run amok

From my huge-hearted Andrew:

I found myself again re-evaluating what was really important to me and the WHY behind my existence which came down to: BE LOVE, no matter what.

I found the woman inside of me that was not only a mother but also a spirit having this human existence. My life didn't happen to me; it happened **for** me to learn, grow, and evolve. I experienced a deeper, more connected relationship with Andrew through "our" journey. He is my best-friend.

I realized that I had the greatest, most supportive partner, John, who would stand beside me and love me even when I "ugly' cried and hated the world.

From both of my sons, I learned that being their mother was the most amazing experience I could have ever chosen without the slightest regret.

Although I love my career path and find my heart is full when helping women just like you release limiting self-beliefs, being "Mom" will always be my greatest achievement.

Lastly, the most important aspect which I found in my story, so far, is that I had an unshakeable belief that Andrew, Jordan, and I were meant to dance this dance called Life together. We were 'destined".

I'm not special nor different from any of you. I didn't have any extraordinary skills to help me through. I just faced what came at me with as much courage as I could muster. As I've told many of my friends, clients, and colleagues, if I can take all this and be like the Phoenix rising, so can they.

During times of deep fear, we have a choice. We can give in, settle for less, be less and expect less. Or we can take the experience and learn from it.

You weren't born to be less than. You weren't born to shrink in order to belong or to be loved. You were born **whole** and nothing that happens to you can change that. You are an expression of pure possibility.

Consider that maybe life isn't about you becoming something but revealing to you, through experiences, who you really are. And that is freeing because you already have everything you need to be you. This is what I found.

I hope my story, which has shaped who I am today, inspires something inside you that says, "I got this", no matter what "this" is. You do! I believe that.

Together, my sons, husband, and I continue to find grace and gratitude.

For life. For each other.

We live.

We learn.

We love.

That's my wish for you.

From my heart to yours.

Rosa Livingstone

...

Erin Hanson

"There is freedom waiting for you,
On the breezes of the sky
And you ask, "What if I fall?"
Oh, but my darling,
What if you fly?"

PART II

More About Women
Like Me

Meet the Authors

SYDNEY MICKEY

A MOMENT IN TIME: LIFE WILL NEVER BE THE SAME

Sydney Mickey grew up in the beautiful northern town of Prince Rupert. Here she has started her new life with her boyfriend and her darling two-month-old son. On top of the world, Sydney never thought the worst could happen, but it did. And she and her family's lives have never been the same since that fateful day.

The accident changed her body for life, Sydney will never walk again. But she never gave up hope and worked hard to recover as much of her life as possible for herself, her son, and her son's father.

Unfortunately, tragedy struck Sydney once again when on June 8, 2019, the love of her life and the father of her son passed away.

Sydney is heading back to school to complete her education. She lives with her four-year-old son and her grandparents in a home located in Langley, British Columbia. She purchased the home, which was already equipped for her needs.

Her father helps out and Sydney is grateful for everyone who has been there for her through her struggles and trauma. Although Sydney is quite independent now and can drive, she still appreciates her family's loving care.

Sydney enjoys the things most young people enjoy and has a supportive group of friends.

There is a sentence that Sydney has on her Facebook page that says all about what an extraordinary young woman she is…

"People stare like they've never seen a goddess in a wheelchair before"

If you would like to contact Sydney, you can reach her by email: Sydney.Victoria.mickey@hotmail.com

———

PAULINE ATITWA

WE HAVE GOD IN HEAVEN: WHO ANSWERS OUR PRAYERS

Pauline Atitwa is founder and Pastor of Neema Word of Life Worship Center in Kaakamega, Mumisa located in Western Kenya. It is here that she does the work of God, helping orphaned children and widows as well as others who are in need.

Pauline is living her passion in life, which is to be of service to others in the world. And she is proud the accomplishments she has achieved during her difficult life.

Pauline lives with her husband and eight children. Six children by birth and two children that she brought home to live with her family because their parents had died and there was no one to care for them. They are now a family of ten, living in one small home. But they all smile, and love fills their home.

Pauline delivers workshops to her widow's group using the Women Like Me books. She focuses on a different woman, from a book each time her group meets. Women are women with the same issues, no matter which part of the world you are from.

Pauline's dream is to help heal the souls of the people she serves. Each person she touches leaves with their heart a bit lighter.

If you would like to reach out to Pauline, you can reach her by email:

paulineatitwa@gmail.com

You can also follow her on Facebook:

https://www.facebook.com/pauline.atitwa.14

―――

DONNA FAIRHURST

PIECES OF MY HEART: SEVEN MIRACLES, TWO ANGELS, AND ONE SACRED SONG FOR LOIS

Donna Fairhurst is a Life and Soul Coach, Author, Reiki Master, and the Chief Evolving officer of Soul Full Solutions, blessed and grateful for the opportunity to share her purpose for being.

Her journey through near blindness, polio, bankruptcy, cancer, multiple near-death experiences, relationship Armageddon, to finally realizing true love taught her to embrace her gifts and her true purpose for BEING. Born and raised in Alberta, Canada, she has travelled the world and studied spiritual and healing modalities for 40 years.

She empowers her clients to pivot powerfully through any challenge and "Live on Purpose" with creativity, and passion. Combining psychic abilities, aura imaging, healing energy modalities, and practical tools for daily living (tough love in a velvet glove), she empowers her clients to their highest level of awareness, here and now.

Visit https://www.DonnaFairhurst.com

- To receive your complimentary Zero 2 Clarity Manifesting and Clearing Prayer
- Or to book an opportunity for a Zero 2 Clarity session

- Read/watch/or listen to radio interviews, podcasts, talks, and articles.
- Live on Purpose with Donna Fairhurst FB Group:

https://www.facebook.com/groups/donnafairhurstlop/?ref=share_group_link

Other Media Links

https://www.facebook.com/SoulFullSolutionsInc/

https://instagram.com/soulfullsolutionsdfairhurst?r=nametag

http://linkedin.com/in/donna-fairhurst-a96733a7

Donna wished to acknowledge and thank every single soul who has contributed in any way to her journey. Namaste

————

TANIA DASHCAVICH

A CHILD OF A SURVIVOR OF A RESIDENTIAL SCHOOL: DO WHAT YOU LOVE, LOVE WHAT YOU DO

Hi, my name is Tania. I am a member of the Athabasca Chipewyan First Nation. My nationality is Cree, dene Ukrainian. I was born and raised in Edmonton, Alberta in, Canada.

My dad is Ukrainian and is from the city of Edmonton. My mother is dene Cree, from Fort Chipewyan. I have just one sibling, and that is my brother.

I am a single mother of four children. Two girls and two boys. I am a baba to two grandchildren. My granddaughter is 13, and my grandson is 10.

Today I live in Fort Chipewyan, which is my mother's hometown. I have been here in Fort chip for about 37 years and work at the Athabasca Delta Community School for helping hands. We promote mental health and well. We hold classes and do community events, all based on mental health, promoting, and sharing awareness.

I love Fort Chipewyan. This is my home. Today I have been sober for 12 years now, and I'm so grateful for my journey. It made me who I am today, and I love who I am.

Thank you for this opportunity, and I wish you all a beautiful journey. And may you find your identity. Because trust me, it does make a difference.

Smudge and Prayers! Marci.

If you would like to reach out to Tania, you can reach her by email at: taniadash01@gmail.com

---

BRENDA-LEE HUOT-HUNTER

WHY EVERY CHILD SHOULD MATTER: ANOTHER STORY OF OUR SHATTERED CHILD WELFARE SYSTEM

Brenda-Lee was raised in Surrey, BC Canada. She often says that "For the most part, I have lived a charmed life". She was raised by great parents who taught her the importance of working in service for others, which led to her calling as a foster parent for over two dozen children.

Beyond the opportunity to open her home and heart for children at a time when they needed it, she also was able to advocate for families and children who were struggling with the child welfare system.

She currently works for an NFP which supports youth and their caregivers, who are experiencing challenges around mental health and substance use issues.

She has been blessed with three daughters, three grandchildren and "the best third husband ever!"

If you would like to reach out to Brenda-Lee, you can contact her at her email: blhunter.est2017@gmail.com

_____

ALISON DEGIANNI

DENYING THE POWER OF GRIEF: RUNNING FROM THE PAIN OF SADNESS

I am a proud wife to Paulo and mother of three adult children, Alissa, Sophia, and Teo. These

beautiful humans encourage me every day to be "ME"! For that, I am forever grateful.

This story is written to show how life's journey takes us down many paths. Most importantly we

have the power and strength to adjust the course.

I am the founder and creative of DeGianni Designs – a boutique interior design studio "Bringing

your story into your home!"

My passion is to create designs that reflect my client's character and style while showcasing their story. We all have one to embrace.

Connect with me

@degiannidesigns – degiannidesigns@gmail.com.

_____

COLINDA LAVIOLETTE

RETURNING TO MY INDIGENOUS CULTURE: HEALED MY HEART

Colinda of Athabasca Chipewyan First Nation of For Chipewyan, Alberta, on Treaty 8 Territory, grew up in a small isolated Indigenous community. She is the mother of six sons, the youngest two of whom live with Down syndrome.

Colinda pursued a career with the GNWT Justice Department within the Corrections Service.

Training in trauma with Dr. Gabor Mate, Colinda shares the knowledge, teachings and education she has acquired throughout this experience. She has found true joy and passion showing others that anything is possible when you believe in yourself.

She is a speaker, writer and has trained as a trauma therapist, working with both western and Indigenous cultural/spiritual practices. She has been featured on CBC Radio, on various panels and is a contributor to "Women Like Me Community: Messages to Younger Self."

An avid podcast guest and presenter, her most recent projects include writing a chapter for a book based on her personal story, being elected to the Board of Directors for Courage in Action and conducting Diversity and Inclusion training on behalf of the Compassionate Inquiry.

In her spare time, she enjoys creating beadwork and facilitating beading workshops.

If you would like to connect, you can reach Colinda by email: jaydar43@hotmail.com

Connect on Facebook: https://www.facebook.com/colinda.laviolette

―――

SABRINA LAMBERT

CULTIVATE RESILIENCE: HEAL FROM THE WOUND, GROW FROM THE SCAR

Sabrina Lambert retired after a successful 39-year career as a corporate training manager.

Presently experiencing an empty nest, she has become a Self Care Strategist and Author. Loving

forest walks, drinking smoothies, and RVing, Sabrina is mom to a grown married daughter, wife to her hubby of three decades, and Gma to her granddaughter.

Discovering the craft of writing in high school, Sabrina used this creativity to publish newsletter articles and employee interest interviews during her corporate career. She is grateful and blessed to write and contribute aspirational works alongside other inspiring authors from the "Women Like Me Community."

When Sabrina is not creating socially distanced Zoom experiences that help her family to stay in touch, she is fine tuning her blueprint for like-minded women who want to embrace the privilege of aging well as a possibility and enjoy fulfillment to make their encore act the best time of their life.

Her Vital Tweaks Framework shows step by step how to integrate essential self care activities into a lifestyle that banishes burnout and sustains vitality. Sabrina mentors and teaches women to

create and implement intentional actions that design their own holistic wellbeing.

Want to contact Sabrina? She would love to connect with you. Here is how you can:

Facebook: https://www.facebook.com/sabrina.self.care

Instagram: https://www.instagram.com/v.sabrinalambert/

Website: https://vitaltweaks.ca

DANA CARTWRIGHT

OBSTACLES: ENDLESS AND IMPOSSIBLE TO CONQUERED

I was born and raised in St. Louis, Missouri and now reside in Lees Summit, a suburb of Kansas City. I live with my husband of 31 years, our 15-year-old boy/girl twins and our multicolored Havanese, Hazel. I love my life.

I am a Registered and Licensed Dietitian by trade and currently use my knowledge and skills as a network marketing professional for a wellness company specializing in nutrigenomics. I love teaching health and prevention! I am passionate about helping people see small tweaks in their health can create big peaks in their focus and energy. I am also super passionate about connections, connecting information to people and connecting people to people.

Helping humans and animals in any capacity is what warms my heart and fills my soul. I find people fascinating and always seek to find the authentic self in others because that is where their best stories and the lessons lie. I believe we are on this earth together to help each other grow into the best possible version of ourselves. I have learned through my many obstacles, there are always solutions to every obstacle and that obstacles precede tremendous growth.

To connect visit:

https://www.facebook.com/dana.cartwright.961

https://www.instagram.com/danakcartwright/

LINDA S. NELSON

SOMEDAY I'LL BE OKAY – BUT SOMEDAY NEVER COMES: IT'S NOT A DATE ON THE CALENDAR

Linda S Nelson is a Business Education graduate and is currently "semi" retired and has recently launched her dream coaching business with her Believe in YOU Academy. She is now able to utilize her experiences and lessons learned throughout her varied career to help people soar from being aimless or unmotivated to finding clarity and confidence and ultimately belief in themselves.

She provides tools and resources along with her coaching to help female solopreneurs rediscover their best selves, identify what holds them back from achieving their very best life, and turn their passions into profit and lead a life of intention and impact.

Her career experiences include Business Teacher, Management Consultant with an executive search firm, Employment Manager for a Fortune 500 company, and human resource consulting, training, and coaching with individuals and numerous organizations. She has been a teacher, stand-up trainer, business owner, marketer, and growth/mindset/belief coach. In addition, she has served on several boards including Board Chair of a state-wide organization that went through intense change under her leadership requiring many shifts in perspective and mindset to survive – and grow.

Linda's strengths include her ability to assess situations and people by asking questions to get to the heart of the matter, developing people and helping organizations and its people grow and offering her unique perspective gained through many years of gathering wisdom from others. Her enthusiasm and belief in "soaring with your strengths" comes through in her pragmatic training/coaching style as she breathes belief in her clients.

Her mission established many years ago is to assist people and organizations in becoming all they can become through their most important asset – the human one – resulting in greater productivity and an increased bottom line. In her "retirement" – she continues with this belief that most of the reason people are not reaching goals as a Solopreneur is because they have neglected their most important asset – themselves.

When Linda is not finding joy in the precious present with her clients, she can be found fully engaged with her loves – gardening and immersing in rich relationships who those important in her life. She lives in Cottonwood MN with the love of her life, Jess and their fur baby, Bella. She and Jess are becoming first-time grandparents at the end of this year – and so will begin traveling to spoil this new wee one and spending time with her only son BJ and the Kelly, his soulmate.

You can Find her on Facebook – Her Profile: Linda Nelson https://www.facebook.com/linda.nelson.399

Her Business Page: Purpose Driven Solopreneur Her Community:

Purpose Seekers Contact her at: Linda@GrowWithLinda.com

ROSA LIVINGSTONE

RAISING MY SONS TWICE: A STORY OF ULTIMATE LOVE

Rosa Livingstone is a Certified Clinical Hypnotherapist, Transformational Mindset, and Life Coach, Speaker, Author of "Self Sabotage: The Art of Screwing Up", "28 Days of Thought-Provoking Power Words, and a contributing Author to "Shine Vol. II".

Rosa has over 15 years of experience coaching and guiding clients to overcome self-sabotaging issues to become the best they can be. Rosa's passion and dedication is very specific: to help other women, at any stage of their life journey, re-discover their authentic selves and rise above limiting beliefs.

Her education, client, and personal experience are the backbone of all her programs, 1:1 coaching, and speaking engagements.

Currently, she offers a Signature Program that helps women acknowledge and release those limiting mindset beliefs so they can move from confusion to clarity and live-out their most passionately purposeful life.

The goal is to move from the fear of 'being herself' to the freedom of embracing **all** of herself. She subscribes to the "Whole-body, Whole-Mind and Whole-life" approach to transformation.

Rosa has financially supported entrepreneurial women through her association with SheEO, a radically generous community supporting women + non-binary people with information and funding worldwide, as well as through her speaking engagements to various organizations including SheTalks Vancouver; Tri-City Women's Networking Organization and as a guest speaking on local radio and television.

She's the mother of two grown Sons and married to the President of her Fanclub, John.

Contact:

(778-238-2427)

www.aloadoffyourmind.com

www.linkedin.com/in/rosa-livingstone-64013422

www.instagram.com/rosalivingstone/

Facebook Private Women's Group: www.facebook.com/groups/transformwithrosa/

...

Helen Keller

"When one door of happiness closes, another opens; but often we look so long at the closed door that we do not see the one which has been opened for us."

Meet Julie Fairhurst

I'm Julie Fairhurst, the Founder of Women Like Me and Story Coach. I want to share with you how Women Like Me came into existence.

When I was ten years old, my mom killed her best friend in a car accident while driving drunk. Three little girls lost their mom that night. And so, did I. My mom didn't physically die. She died inside and was never the same again.

Her life spiraled down due to shame and unbelievable guilt, and she took her children with her.

Drug addiction and alcoholism became rapid in my family. My siblings and myself were thrown into a life of chaos. It was entirely out of control.

I became pregnant at 14 years of age, married at 17, divorced at 29, and a single mother with three young children and a grade eight education. I thought my life was set for failure, following down my parents' path. I was headed in the wrong direction.

But, somewhere deep inside, that young girl inside showed up and reminded me that I wanted better for my life and the life of my children. I had no support from anyone, not a soul. I had to do it all on my own.

Was it an easy road? No, it was far from easy. I was a single mom for 24 years. We lived off government handouts. I stood in line at food banks to feed my kids. At Christmas, we received Christmas hampers, and I would go to the toy bank to get presents for the kids. The path we were on was not easy to change, especially when it was all you knew.

But I did it. I went back to school and finished my education. I built an outstanding career in sales, marketing and promotion. I won the company's top awards and was the first woman to achieve top sales-people year after year in a male-dominated industry. I was able to buy a home on my own and provide a stable environment to raise my children.

Some people say never to look back, but I do every day. Why? Because I never want to forget the journey that led me to where I am today. And today, my life is entirely different. I didn't just fall into this life. I worked at it every day, all the time.

Then, in 2019, my beautiful 24-year-old niece died from a drug overdose on the streets of Vancouver, Canada. And that was the day I said enough! My niece's death indirectly resulted from my mother's actions or non-actions and my siblings continuing with their destructive lifestyles.

When we don't deal with our traumas, we pass the dysfunction along to the next generation and the next. This is where my passion comes from, the reason I started Women Like Me. But I am only one person.

Now I am reaching out to you, you who would be in service of others, healers, coaches, and anyone who deals with the public personally. If you work with the public, you may not think you can help them change their lives, but you can.

I have started a movement, but I can't do it alone. It's time to share your stories with others to inspire change in their lives and help us all along our way.

Want to reach out? There are many ways to find me.

Email: julie@changeyourpath.ca

Women Like Me Stories

www.womenlikemestories.com

Find me on Social Media:

Rock Star Strategies on Facebook

https://www.facebook.com/juliefairhurstcoaching

LinkedIn

https://www.linkedin.com/in/womenlikemestories/

Instagram

https://www.instagram.com/womenlikemestories/

Want to buy books and support our women authors? There are two ways to do that.

Women Like Me Books

https://womenlikemestories.com/buy-books/

Amazon – search Julie Fairhurst in the search bar or go here…

https://www.amazon.com/s?k=julie+fairhurst&ref=nb_sb_noss

...

Eleanor Roosevelt

"A woman is like a tea bag; you never know how strong it is until it's in hot water."

Join The Women Like Me Community

If you do not belong to Women Like Me Community – Julie Fairhurst, I would be pleased if you decided to join us.

The Women Like Me Community – Julie Fairhurst is a Facebook group of like-minded women. Women who want to pay it forward and lift others up to promote healing in the world. Ages range from 17 to 83 years of age from all over the world and from all walks of life.

As a community, we write community books, with the proceeds going to charity. Maybe you will join in on the next book?

Together, as a group, we can help promote healing in our world.

Join the Movement on Facebook:

Come to the community and spent time with other inspiring women. We are waiting for you!

Women Like Me Community – Julie Fairhurst

https://www.facebook.com/groups/879482909307802

...

Kavia Ramdas

"We need women who are so strong they can be gentle, so educated they can be humble, so fierce they can be compassionate, so passionate they can be rational, and so disciplined they can be free."

Would you like to be an author in the book series?

Do you have a story that needs to be told? A story that may be holding you back from living your best life? Or possibly, you have overcome and are ready to share with the world, hoping that your story will invoke another to live a better life?

Writing is therapeutic to the soul. Writing about your past events can be beneficial, both emotionally and physically. You can increase your feelings of well-being and even enhance your immune system.

We only get one chance. Our lives are not a dress rehearsal for our next lifetime. We only get this one life, and it's here, and it's now.

Reach out to me at www.womelikemestories.com and let me know you are ready to tell your story. The world is waiting for you.

Women Like Me Academy
FOR WOMEN IN BUSINESS

There is massive power in stories! And, in your story!

Have you ever noticed that many celebrities repeat parts of their stories in almost every interview they do? That's because there is immense power in our stories. But it needs to be the right story that will align with your business.

In the academy, we will flush out your story. Once you've written your chapter in the book, we will move to promote you and your story to the world.

Your prospective clients will be drawn to you because you will connect to them through your story. You will leave the academy with promotional pieces that you can use to promote your story, your business, and you personally.

If you would like to learn more about the academy, you can reach me at julie@changeyourpath.ca

...

Michelle Obama

"There is no limit to what we, as women, can accomplish."

Other Books by Julie Fairhurst

Women Like Me Book Series

- Women Like Me – A Celebration of Courage and Triumphs
- Women Like Me – Stories of Resilience and Courage
- Women Like Me – A Tribute to the Brave and Wise
- Women Like Me – Breaking Through the Silence

———

Women Like Me Community Book Series

- Women Like Me Community – Messages To My Younger Self
- Women Like Me Community – Sharing Words Of Gratitude
- Women Like Me Community – Sharing What We Know To Be True

———

Mindset

- Your Mindset Matters
- Build Your Self-Esteem – 100 Tips designed to boost your confidence

- Self-Esteem Journal

- Agent Etiquette – 14 Things You Didn't Learn in Real Estate School
- 7 Keys to Success – How to Become a Real Estate Sales Badass
- Net Marketing
- 30 Days To Real Estate Action
- 100 Reasons Agents Quit The Business

Acknowledgments

A special thank you to all my 11 Authors of Women Like me – From Loss To Living. It has been an honor to work with you, and to get to know each one of you personally. You are indeed, an amazing and caring group of women.

When the Women Like Me books are being writing, the subtitle is always chosen after the stories have been written. The subtitle of this book From Loss To Living is exactly what everyone of you have done.

Not one of your stories are the same. Each of you have experiences different struggles in life, and each one of you have overcome. And you are wiser and stronger for it.

Opening up about the traumas we experience in our lives, growing up and as adults can be difficult to share. Some things we'd rather, keep pushed down deep inside our souls, hopefully keeping them there for our entire lives.

But the universe doesn't work that way. We are meant to grow, evolve, and overcome. So, we can pass along our lessons and wisdom to help others who are hurting in the world. We are meant to heal, so others can heal as well.

I celebrate all of you for your growth, openness, and ability to share your stories. It is not easy, but each one of you went deep inside and brought out beautiful stories during the process of writing for Women Like Me. It is a complicated process, but you all did it and should be very proud of accomplishments.

With so my gratitude for you all,

Your friend Julie

...

Amy Schumer

"I am a woman with thoughts and questions and sh*t to say. I say if I'm beautiful. I say if I'm strong. You will not determine my story – I will."

To you, the reader

I appreciate your support. It means everything to the authors and, of course, to me.

It is a daunting task to write about your personal life, especially when there is trauma, illness, and inner work that the writers are describing. It is vulnerable to put themselves out there and share their personal lives with the world.

I can honestly tell you, each of the women who wrote their story in Women Like Me does it because they understand that others are in need, and they hope through telling their story, that woman will read their story and decide for themselves to live their best lives.

Every writer asks me, "do you think my story will help others." And I tell them YES!

Of course, they write for other personal reasons, but knowing that they can help another by telling their story to heal their life is at the forefront of their minds as they write.

If you felt a women's story in the book helped you along your path in life, you can go and leave a message. I will be sure to pass it along to the author. It would be my pleasure to do that for you.

www.womenlikemestories.com

Made in the USA
Columbia, SC
06 September 2022

66680990R00117